WORLD WAR II

The Road to Dunkirk

BROWN REFERENCE GROUP

The Brown Reference Group, Ltd
First Floor, 9–17 St Albans Place
London N1 0NX

Editorial Director:	Lindsey Lowe
Editor:	Pete Darman
Managing Editor:	Deborah Evans
Design Manager:	Jeni Child
Designers:	Jerry Udell, John Dinsdale
Picture Researcher:	Andrew Webb
Production Director:	Alastair Gourlay
Production:	Richard Berry

Picture Credits: Front Cover: Getty Images/Hulton (top left); Robert Hunt Library (top right, bottom left, bottom right, centre). All other images: Robert Hunt Library, except Topfoto, p.71.

Printed in Italy

ISBN 978 1 84044 323 3

CONTENTS

Chapter 1
Hitler's Rise to Power

Resentful of the peace treaties of 1919 and split by political extremism, postwar Germany provided an ideal stage for a charismatic politician to rise to power on a platform of nationalism, militarism and intolerance. Manipulating democratic politics to get into power, Hitler then ruthlessly created a dictatorship and began planning wars of conquest.

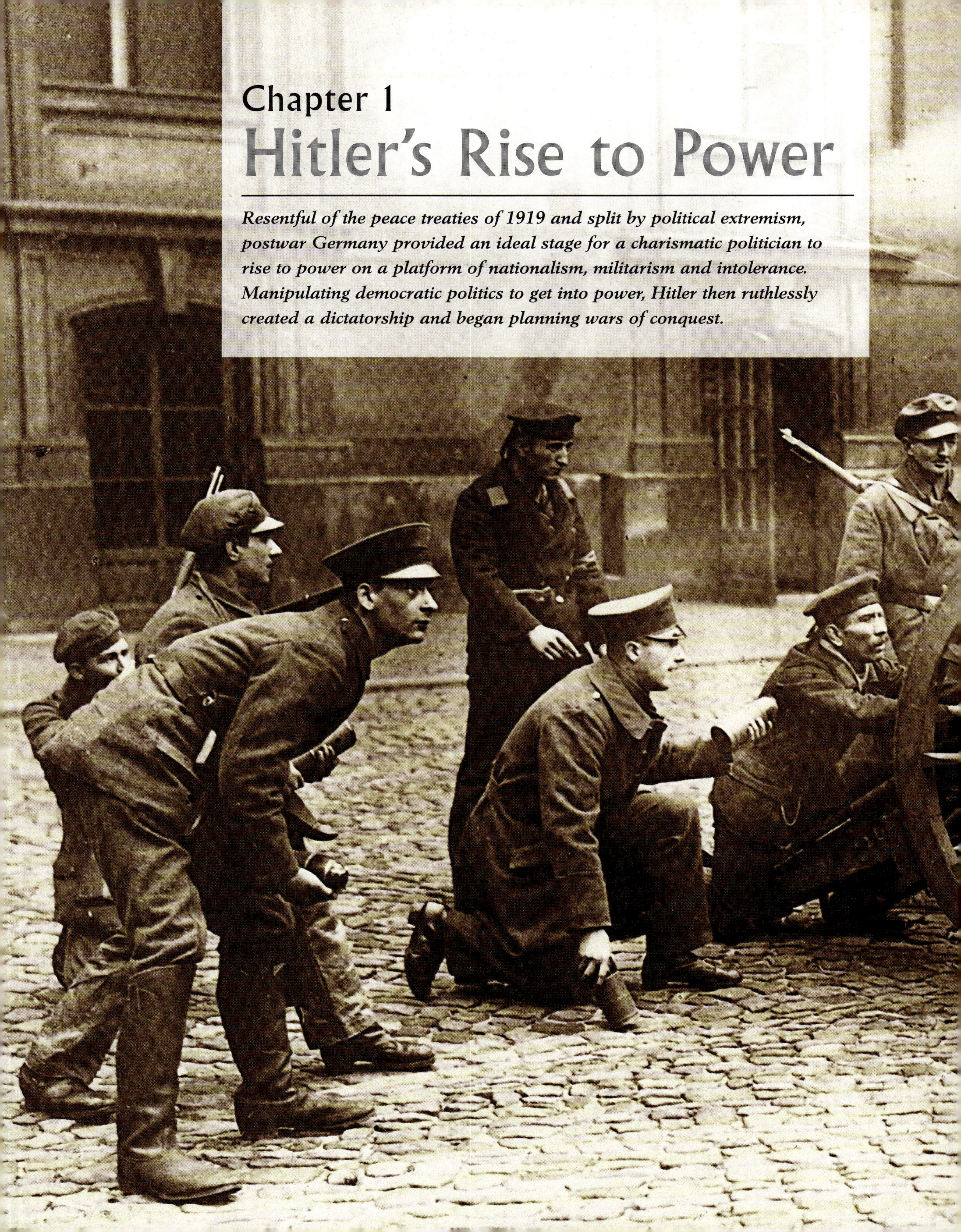

Previous pages: German sailors and soldiers during the attempted revolution in 1919.

In October 1918, a key Allied condition for peace negotiations was that Kaiser Wilhelm should abdicate. He did so on 9 November, ending the monarchy in Germany. The country was proclaimed a republic, and two days later the civilian government signed the armistice ending World War I. But by that point, Germany was already very unstable. Instability and weak government bedevilled the country for over a decade, until Hitler came to power in 1933.

At the start of November 1918, a naval mutiny turned into a widespread revolt. Workers set up councils in many cities. Political violence erupted on the streets. In December 1918, the extreme left formed the German Communist Party (KPD). Next month the German Workers' Party (DAP) was set up on the extreme right. It was this party – later the National Socialist German Workers' Party (NSDAP), or the Nazis – that World War I veteran Adolf Hitler joined in September 1919.

The Weimar Republic

In January 1919, the communist Spartacus League staged a coup in the capital, Berlin. Four months later, the state of Bavaria declared itself a soviet republic. Both risings were put down by right-wing paramilitaries sent in by the government. Known as *Freikorps*, these groups of ex-servicemen proved hard to control.

Against this background an assembly met to draw up a new constitution. Because Berlin was unsafe, it met in the city of Weimar. Historians refer to the government it created as the Weimar Republic. Its early years were marked by short-lived coalitions. While elections took place, uprisings continued. In March

A Workers' Defence Force militia unit deployed for action, somewhere in Germany in 1921.

1920, a right-wing coup failed to take power in Berlin. Political killings were also common during this period. In June 1922, for example, anti-semitic nationalists killed Germany's Jewish foreign minister, Walther Rathenau.

First appearance of the Nazis

In 1920, the NSDAP issued its political platform, which included the rejection of the Versailles treaty, German territorial expansion, and the disbarment of Jews from citizenship. The next year Hitler became chairman and organized the party's private army, the *Sturmabteilung* (SA). Labelled the Brownshirts, the SA roamed the streets fighting with opponents.

> "A naval mutiny turned into a widespread revolt"

Over the next few years, the fledgling Weimar Republic struggled against pressures both within and without Germany. A major problem it faced was the fact that it accepted that Germany had caused World War I, and that the Allied powers had the right to be paid reparations by Germany. However, the perception of many in Germany was that Versailles was unfair. It was, in their eyes, a punitive "Carthaginian Peace" designed to crush German strength for ever. There were those in Britain, such as the economist John Maynard Keynes, who supported this view in books such as *The Economic Consequences of the Peace*, published in 1919. For a population trying to come to terms with defeat and economic depression, the idea of a punitive peace soon took hold. Many in Germany even questioned whether they had been defeated at all. After all, Germany was not occupied when the war ended in November 1918, and the German Army had withdrawn from the front in France and Belgium at the war's

Hitler using his considerable speech-making skills at a meeting in Germany in the interwar years.

BENITO MUSSOLINI

Mussolini's rise to power in Italy preceded Hitler's in Germany by 11 years, and in the 1920s Mussolini was Europe's leading fascist dictator. He began his career as a socialist, but in World War I saw that the nationalist right offered a surer route to power. In 1921 he was elected to parliament, with 34 other fascist deputies. He moved to consolidate fascism by founding the National Fascist Party (PNF). Coming to power in October 1922, he manipulated the 1924 elections to seize absolute power. Mussolini gave himself the title of *Il Duce* (the leader) in 1925.

For five years, Mussolini oversaw a social and economic revolution intended to make the state and its leader the focus of the nation's efforts. From the mid-1930s, he boosted his popularity by a series of foreign wars. Intervention in the Spanish Civil War in 1936, however, drew the regime into alliance with Germany, which led to Italy's disastrous entry into World War II. In July 1943 Mussolini was overthrown. He survived with Hitler's help until April 1945, when he was captured and executed by communist partisans.

Hitler addressing a Nazi Party rally in the palace park at Tiefurt. These early rallies were a foretaste of the well-planned rallies after the Nazis came to power in 1933.

end in good order. This was the "Stab-in-the-Back" myth that proved very potent in all sections of German society: the idea that it was Marxists and Jews on the home front who had betrayed the army.

Germany was forced to forfeit all of its overseas empire by the Versailles Treaty, and had lost much territory in Europe. A major part of the western Germany, the Rhineland, was placed under international control, while a major part of the new Germany, East Prussia, was separated from the rest of Germany by land allocated to the newly reconstituted nation of Poland.

The reparations themselves were fixed at $26 billion, a huge sum. When the German Government was unable to pay in 1923, French troops occupied parts of the Ruhr, one of Germany's main industrial areas.

Soon, Germany was in the grip of a growing economic crisis. It suffered a catastrophic inflationary spiral. A loaf of bread that cost half a mark (Germany's currency) in December 1918 cost 163 marks by December 1922, 1465 marks by June 1923, and 201 billion marks that November. This hyperinflation wiped out savings. It made many people bitter at the government's inability to solve the problem, and further undermined the legitimacy of the Weimer Republic.

Hitler's move for power

Hitler moved to take advantage of the unpopularity of the government. On 9 November 1923, he led an uprising, or putsch, in Munich to take control of the Bavarian government. The putsch failed and Hitler was jailed. However, his trial gave him a platform to push the Nazis into the public eye. The failure of the putsch had another important result. It convinced Hitler that violence alone would not bring him to power, and that he needed to work within the democratic system for the time being.

For the rest of the decade, Hitler concentrated on building electoral support. Meanwhile the liberal government of

MEIN KAMPF

Mein Kampf is a mixture of autobiography and political ideas. Hitler dictated the book in prison after the failed Beer Hall Putsch of 1923. The book outlined Hitler's beliefs and political programme. It clearly displayed all his prejudices. He created a racial hierarchy in which Germans were at the top and Jews at the bottom. Hitler blamed the Jews for Germany's problems. He claimed that they were intent on world domination and were trying to pollute "superior" races by marrying into them. He also ranted against communism, democratic government and capitalism.

The book outlined Hitler's projected programme in the wider world, much of which later took place. He believed that Germany needed more territory and that it would acquire it by military action. The book predicted rearmament, the rejection of the Versailles Treaty, and war with France and the Soviet Union.

Berlin Jews gather in the street. The economic problems Germany experienced in the interwar period allowed the Nazis to whip up anti-semitism as part of their racist policies and the search for scapegoats.

Gustav Stresemann ended hyperinflation by introducing a new currency, and the Weimar Republic became more stable.

Calm before the storm

Germany's economic recovery was aided by the start in fall 1924 of the Dawes Plan. The plan rearranged Germany's reparations payments and allowed for huge US loans to help pay them. The period of relative recovery continued with the signing of the Treaty of Locarno in October 1925. Germany accepted its western boundaries as laid down in the Versailles Treaty. In return, Germany was allowed to join the League of Nations the following year.

In 1929, the Young Plan (named for US businessman Owen D. Young) cut reparations to around 25 percent of the 1921 demand. Hitler supported a nationalist campaign against the plan, because it still followed the terms of the hated Versailles Treaty. In December 1929, however, a large majority of Germans voted to accept the plan. It seemed that Germany had no desire for the nationalists or the NSDAP.

> "In autumn 1929, a crisis of confidence hit the USA"

Events elsewhere, however, were soon to change the situation dramatically. In autumn 1929, a crisis of confidence hit the USA. It sparked US investors to begin selling their stocks and shares. The selling turned into a panic, culminating in Black Tuesday, 29 October. More than 16 million shares were sold, wiping billions

Members of the Brownshirts at a torchlight parade. Torn between violent political extremes and attracted by Hitler's self assurance, young men joined the Brownshirts in their thousands during the 1930s.

of dollars from the worth of US corporations. The United States raised tariffs, or taxes on imports, to protect its industry. Other nations followed suit, and the new tariffs effectively stifled international trade. The resulting global slump was a major cause of the Great Depression, a long period of great economic hardship.

Nowhere was this hardship felt more than in Germany. The country's economic well-being depended on US loans that soon dried up. German companies went bankrupt, laying off millions of workers. In December 1929, unemployment in Germany stood at 1.8 million. By early 1933, it had reached more than 6 million. That was a quarter of the labour force. Over a similar period industrial output fell by around 40 percent. Once again, ordinary Germans felt that the Weimar republic had failed them. Many looked for an alternative to extremist parties such as Hitler's NSDAP.

Hitler's appeal

As in the early 1920s, Hitler's policies struck a chord with wide sections of the public. The middle classes, for example, had been financially hard hit for the second time in less than a decade. Even moderate Germans resented the Treaty of Versailles. Hitler appealed to them with his promise to restore Germany to its correct position in the world. At the same time he blamed Germany's problems on an alliance of Jews, communists and bankers. These scapegoats drew on stereotypes familiar in German culture. Hitler's powerful arguments, plus a careful use of propaganda, brought the Nazi Party rapid success. It had won only 12 seats in the 1928 election to the Reichstag (parliament). In September

German girls practise the Nazi salute in the town of Coburg. Women had a particular place in Nazi ideology: mainly to stay in the home and produce children.

THE GREAT DEPRESSION

Extremism in Europe was intensified by the hardship that resulted from the Great Depression of the 1930s. The financial crash that struck Wall Street in October 1929 was disastrous for European nations reliant on US trade and loans.

Germany soon felt the effects as the United States called in its loans and cut back its imports. By 1932 German industrial production had fallen by 46 percent. People whose lives were ruined by the economic collapse began to look to the far right for answers.

Elsewhere, too, people saw democratic politics as a cause of the crisis. Dictators took power in smaller countries, such as António Salazar in Portugal and Ioannis Metaxas in Greece, by promising to control the economic chaos in their countries.

The crisis seemed to vindicate Mussolini's fascists in Italy, who in the mid-1920s had brought the economy largely under government control. Some observers saw Italy's success in avoiding the worst of the Depression as proof that fascism worked. Austria, for example, reorganized its industry in a similar model of state corporations.

Dr Josef Goebbels casts his vote in Berlin, 1933. The organizational abilities of Hitler's propaganda supremo gave the Nazi Party many votes in the elections of the 1920s.

1930, however, the NSDAP won 107 seats. It became the second-largest party, behind the moderate Social Democrats (SPD) who were in power.

Manoeuvring for power

No party had a parliamentary majority, making the passage of new laws difficult. As in any economic crisis, the ruling party, in this case the SPD, found itself unpopular in trying to control the economy in a devastating world downturn.

The Weimar constitution gave considerable power to the president, who in this period was Field Marshal Paul von Hindenburg, head of the army at the end of World War I, and no friend of liberal politicians.

In April 1932, Hitler stood against Hindenburg in the presidential election and won 37 percent of the vote. Chancellor Heinrich Brüning feared that the Nazis were about to try to seize power in a coup. Three days after the presidential election, he banned the Nazis' private armies: the SA and the *Schutzstaffel* (SS). The SS had been formed in 1925 as a bodyguard for Hitler. Brüning's move was unpopular conservative Germans. In late May, Hindenburg replaced Brüning with the conservative Franz von Papen.
In return for Hitler's support, Papen lifted the ban on the Nazis' private armies. Street battles broke out between

Eyewitness Report:

"There were quite a few Storm Troopers who had Jewish girlfriends and therefore a lot of Germans just thought, 'Oh well, it's not going to be so bad – they have Jewish girlfriends they can't hate us all.' A Nazi said to me, 'You really should be one of us.' I said, 'Look, I can't, I'm a Jew,' and he would say: 'We don't mean you, decent chaps like you will be perfectly all right in the new Germany.'"

Eugene Leviné, a Jew and communist, 1933

the SA and SS on the one hand and communist paramilitaries on the other. Papen called a national election for 31 July 1932. In the election, Hitler's NSDAP emerged as the largest party, with 37.3 percent of the vote and 230 seats. Hindenburg offered Hitler the post of vice-chancellor. Hitler insisted upon becoming chancellor; Hindenburg refused. Papen kept the job, but in the autumn the Reichstag passed a vote of no confidence in him. Fresh elections were called for November.

A fateful misjudgment

In the 6 November election, the Nazis lost ground to the communists. They remained the largest party in the Reichstag, however, with 196 seats. Hindenburg still would not make Hitler chancellor. Instead he appointed General Kurt von Schleicher to the post. Schleicher had no more support in parliament than Papen. His administration was over in 57 days.

In early January 1933, Papen met with Hitler. He proposed a coalition government, with Hitler as chancellor and himself as vice chancellor. Papen convinced Hindenburg that, with only three Nazis in the government, Hitler could be kept in check. Hindenburg finally agreed to make Hitler chancellor. The fatal miscalculation of Germany's conservative right was to believe that Hitler could be controlled once in power.

Hitler consolidates power

Once he had become chancellor, Hitler moved swiftly to secure the Nazis' hold on power. Although there were only three Nazi politicians in the national

THE GERMAN COMMUNIST PARTY

The German Communist Party (KPD) was the largest communist party outside the Soviet Union after the end of World War I. The party was highly active, leading the Spartacist uprising of January 1919 and forming a soviet republic in Bavaria in April. In the early years of the Weimar Republic, the KPD fared better in the elections than Hitler's Nazi Party, but from 1930 onwards it lost ground. Under the leadership of Ernst Thälmann the KPD waged war on the moderate socialists of the SPD, preventing the political left uniting against Hitler. In 1933, after the Reichstag building was set on fire by a communist, Hitler outlawed the Communist Party. Under the Nazis thousands of KPD members were jailed, exiled or killed.

Hitler with the German President Paul von Hindenburg. Germany's ruling élite hoped to control Hitler and use him to smash the forces of revolution.

Germans holidaying on the Baltic coast during the 1930s. Ordinary German workers found their living conditions improved enormously under the Nazi regime.

cabinet, Hermann Göring, one of the key Nazi leaders, was minister of the interior in Prussia, which included the main German city, Berlin, a key communist stronghold. In February, Göring purged the Prussian police of any left-wing sympathizers, and then enlisted 40,000 Nazis as auxiliaries to crush any resistance to the Nazis.

Hitler called an election for March and events played into his hands perfectly. On 27 February 1933, a fire was started in the Reichstag by a communist arsonist. The new chancellor was able to suspend civil liberties and ban the German Communist Party (KPD). The episode enabled the Nazis to stir up fear of the communist threat during the election campaign. It also supported Hitler's insistence on an Enabling Act, which would make the chancellor all powerful, to protect the nation.

In the 5 March election, the NSDAP increased its number of seats to 288. It lacked an overall majority, but by alliances and intimidation, Hitler got the Enabling Act passed on 23 March.

Hitler soon used his new dictatorial powers. In a bid to crush political opposition, between March and July 1933 he outlawed all parties other than the NSDAP, and also abolished trade unions. He began locking up his political opponents in SA-run concentration camps. By the end of 1933 there were about 150,000 prisoners in such camps, the most important of which was at Dachau, near Munich. Meanwhile, the Nazis

The Reichstag arsonist, a simple-minded Dutchman named Marinus van der Lubbe, stands trial for arson. He was executed, but it has never been fully established whether he was really to blame or whether he was a scapegoat.

SA men round up suspected communists during the reign of terror that began in 1933 when SA members were recruited by Göring as police auxiliaries.

extended their control over all areas of life. The Gestapo (secret police) was set up in April 1933 to monitor and arrest potential opponents of the regime, while the Nazis also took over the media, closely controlling the output of the German cinema industry, closing down liberal or Jewish-owned newspapers, and allowing no voices of dissent on the national radio. Particularly noteworthy in the 1930s were the attacks on modern art and the public burning of books that the Nazis disagreed with.

Purges and murder

As the Nazis tightened their grip on Germany, however, divisions appeared in the party itself. In summer 1934, Hitler became concerned about the leftish politics of senior officers in the SA, which was now four million strong, and in particular of its leader, Ernst Röhm. He and many of his followers wanted a further radicalization of Germany, to include state control of private enterprise and SA control of the army. Röhm had powerful enemies in the army and in the Nazi Party itself, including SS chief Heinrich Himmler. Himmler and high-ranking Nazi Hermann Göring convinced Hitler that Röhm was planning a coup.

On the night of 29–30 June 1934, Nazi police and the SS rounded up Röhm and other SA officers. Many, including Röhm,

> **"The Night of the Long Knives shocked and terrified the German public"**

were executed. Hitler also rid himself of other potential opponents, among them former chancellor Schleicher. The so-called Night of the Long Knives, during which perhaps 1000 people died, shocked and terrified the German public.

Members of the SA pass a set of posters with crude Jewish stereotypes. Der Sturmer *was a weekly Nazi newspaper that specialized in such images. It was said to be the only newspaper that Hitler read from cover to cover.*

In August, following the death of Hindenburg, Hitler strengthened his own position. He merged the posts of president and chancellor into a single office. Hitler took the title of Führer (leader) – and with it absolute power in Germany. Further constitutional changes included changing the federal structure of Germany into one unitary state.

Religion was an area that Hitler was also determined to control. An agreement with the Pope in 1933 meant that Catholic criticism was effectively silenced, and when Protestant opposition surfaced it was swiftly dealt with. Late in 1935, 700 Protestant pastors were arrested. The following year, over 800 more were taken into custody for protesting at attacks on churches and anti-semitism.

Anti-semitism had been a key part of Nazi ideology since the early 1920s, and Hitler began to take action against Germany's Jews soon after taking power. The German Jewish community was 650,000 strong in 1933, and had been the victim of direct Nazi attacks since 1930. Synagogues and cemeteries had been targets for SA violence and some Jews actually murdered. Once Hitler became chancellor, such violence escalated. Then, in April 1933, Hitler instituted a boycott of Jewish businesses.

German students and Nazi paramilitaries burn so-called un-German books in Berlin in May 1933. A band played as 20,000 books were destroyed.

Eyewitness Report:

"We had three elderly ladies who were living on the first floor with us. One was dragged out and beaten up for no reason except that she got in the way or something. I was knocked about and finally ended up in the cellar ... I was absolutely in shock. I couldn't understand how this situation had arisen. It was uncalled for violence against a people they didn't know."

Rudi Bamber, nine years old at the time of *Kristallnacht*

He went on to enact a series of laws against the Jewish community, including the Nuremberg Laws of 1935. This set of measures stripped Jews of their German citizenship, forbade marriage between Jews and others, and barred Jews from the professions (and most other forms of employment).

The worst single incidence of Nazi anti-semitism during the period before 1939 was *Kristallnacht* – the Night of Broken Glass. In retaliation for the murder of a German diplomat in Paris by a Polish Jew, Nazi storm troopers raided and destroyed Jewish homes and businesses in an orgy of violence. Nearly 200 synagogues were burnt down. What little rights Germany's Jews still possessed were then rescinded. By 1939, over 400,000 Jews had emigrated. Most of those that remained then died in the greater horror of the Holocaust in World War II.

An economic miracle?

While many Germans protested at Hitler's racial policies, many more did not. This was partly because the police state that had been set up made any sign of dissent very dangerous; but it was also true that many Germans did well out of the new regime. Many army officers were enthusiastic supporters of his decision to rearm; similarly, industrialists did well under Hitler, as did their employees.

Hitler put Hjalmar Schlact in charge of the economy soon after he came to power. Schlact put people to work by implementing a programme of public works and borrowing heavily. A new motorway system of autobahns was built, for example. Within two years, Schlact had reduced unemployment from six million to under three million. He resigned in 1937, but a policy of sustained rearmament under Hermann Göring then kept the German economy booming. The boom could certainly not have continued for much longer than

SPOTLIGHT

The Hitler Youth

Hitler was determined to spread Nazi ideology among the young people of Germany. The Hitler Youth was the most important expression of this drive.

By the end of 1933, all other youth organizations (apart from some Catholic groups) had been either banned or subsumed into the Hitler Youth. By early 1934, nearly half of boys between 10 and 14 were in the Hitler Youth, while 15 percent of girls between those ages were in its female equivalent, the Young Girls' League. This was a sustained attempt to indoctrinate the young people of Germany.

Far left: Baldur von Schirach, Reich Youth Leader. A devoted admirer of Hitler, he was appointed head of the Hitler Youth in 1933.

Above: Members of the Hitler Youth eating outdoors. In some ways, the Hitler Youth was the equivalent of the Boy Scout movement in the UK.

Below left: A Hitler Youth rally in Germany in the 1930s.

Below: A Hitler Youth marching practice. Where the Hitler Youth was unlike the Boy Scout movement was in its emphasis on military skills.

Above right: A group of Hitler Youth are shown the workings of a machine gun. The organization was designed in part to act as a form of military training.

Right: More explicit military training with rifles on the firing range in the 1930s.

Below right: A map reading exercise for young Germans. in 1933, Hitler described how he wanted a new generation "swift as the greyhound, tough as leather, and hard as Krupp steel".

A Nazi rally at Nuremberg in 1934. In the centre of the picture are Hitler (middle), Heinrich Himmler (left, the head of the SS) and Victor Lutze (right, chief of the SA).

1939, but during the mid-1930s the average German worker felt much better off than during the period 1930–33.

It was not just secure employment that made the German worker feel good about the Nazi regime. The unions may have been banned, but workers became members of the German Labour Front (German acronym DAF), which organised holidays with travel expenses and workers' education programmes.

Strength Through Joy

The Strength Through Joy holiday movement, heavily funded by the Nazis, also offered holidays to ordinary Germans for the first time. Hundreds of thousands of Germans went on cruises on luxury liners (two of which were built specially for Strength Through Joy).

It was not only industrial workers who enjoyed prosperity under Nazi rule. The peasant farmers of Germany were given priority by the new regime, and although the results were not as successful as in heavy industry, the countryside was generally happy under Nazi rule.

Economic well being was supplemented by something wider: a sense that Germany would now achieve its proper place in the world, a place denied it during the Weimar Republic. The great rallies of the mid-1930s, especially those held at at Nuremberg, grandiose building projects under architect Albert Speer, the hosting of the Olympic Games in 1936, and Hitler's decision to ignore the Versailles Treaty and rearm the German military enthused German nationalists. They were even more encouraged by Hitler's decision to expand Germany's role on the international stage and to overturn the Versailles Treaty entirely. They were not to know that this would lead to eventual catastrophe.

SA men stick propaganda posters on a store during a boycott of Jewish businesses in 1933. The Nazis began to encourage German anti-semitism almost as soon as they took power.

NUREMBERG RALLIES

Held for the first time in 1923, the party rally of the NSDAP settled in Nuremberg from 1927. Lasting for several days in September, the rally was a meticulously organized theatrical spectacle designed to show off the power and sense of unity of the German people and their Nazi ideology. The programme included torchlit rallies, speeches by party leaders to massed audiences, and parades in front of Hitler himself. As up to 500,000 of the party faithful from all over Germany gathered to pledge their loyalty to the Führer, the rally could take on an almost religious quality. Josef Goebbels, the Nazi propaganda specialist, referred to the event as "the High Mass of our party". The Nuremberg rallies were filmed and shown in German cinemas and at party gatherings. The most famous example is Leni Riefenstahl's movie documentary of the 1934 rally, *Triumph of the Will*. The Nuremberg rallies ceased after 1938, the 1939 event being cancelled because of the outbreak of World War II.

Chapter 2

Europe in Crisis: 1935–1939

As Hitler's position grew more secure within Germany, he began a campaign of territorial expansion that was initially met with inaction by France and Britain but eventually drove the continent to war.

Adolf Hitler made no secret of his opposition to the 1919 Treaty of Versailles, which limited Germany's armed forces, and had reduced Germany in size. Many Germans shared his resentment at the treaty. They thought it was unjustifiably harsh. As early as February 1933, Hitler shared with his generals a plan to take back the Sudetenland – a German-speaking area of Czechslovakia – and make a union with Austria, before defeating France, Poland and Russia. Few of his listeners took him seriously. Within a few years, however, it would become clear that Hitler was deadly serious.

International relations

In October 1933, Hitler took Germany out of the permanent disarmament talks in Geneva and the League of Nations, the body set up to solve international disputes. Hitler signed a nonaggression pact with his eastern neighbour, Poland, in January 1934, removing any danger of a pre-emptive Polish strike on Germany.

Suspicion

Hitler also sought to make alliances within Europe. The most obvious ally was Italy, governed by Benito Mussolini. There were parallels between Mussolini's fascism and Hitler's Nazism, and the Italians also resented Versailles, which they felt had failed to reward them for their part in the Allied victory. Mussolini also rejected the League of Nations. When he invaded Abyssinia (Ethiopia) in October 1935, he ignored its protests.

The alliance between Hitler and Mussolini started badly, however. Mussolini was not impressed by Hitler,

Previous pages: A mass Nazi Party rally at Nuremberg in the 1930s.

British prime minister Neville Chamberlain (centre right) and German foreign minister Joachim von Ribbentrop (right) review a guard of honour at the Munich Conference in September 1938. French and British concessions at the conference failed to stop Europe's slide towards war.

and was suspicious of Hitler's plan to create a Greater Germany. Hitler envisaged an *Anschluss*, or union, with Austria, Italy's northern neighbour. Mussolini wanted to keep Austria independent as a buffer between Italy and Germany.

On 25 July 1934, Austrian Nazis, with Hitler's support, murdered the Austrian chancellor, Engelbert Dollfuss, a fierce opponent of the *Anschluss*, during a failed coup. Mussolini mobilized his army on the Austrian border, ready to support the government against Nazi aggression. Kurt von Schuschnigg, a pro-Italian fascist, became the new chancellor. To some observers in France and Britain, it seemed that Mussolini could be a useful block to Hitler's territorial expansionism.

The Saarland and Stresa

In January 1935, the people of the Saarland, a southwestern region that had been removed from Germany by the Versailles treaty, voted to rejoin Germany. The result was celebrated as a victory for German nationalism.

In March 1935, Hitler announced that Germany would no longer accept the military limitations of Versailles. In fact rearmament had been going on for two years. By 1935, for example, the German army had increased from 100,000 to 300,000 men, while the air force – actually forbidden by Versailles – consisted of 18,000 personnel and hundreds of aircraft. Hitler was hoping that he could disregard Versailles with little danger of provoking other European powers into action.

The Stresa Front

In response to German rearmament, Mussolini called a conference with France and Britain at the Italian city of Stresa in April 1935. The so-called Stresa Front agreed to use force to defend the Versailles Treaty. The agreement soon fell apart, however, when Hitler offered to make nonaggression pacts with his

German troops cross the River Rhine during the reoccupation of the Rhineland on 7 March 1936. Hitler later said that waiting to see whether the Allies would call his bluff and move against him was one of the worst times of his life.

Adolf Hitler and Nazi naval chief Admiral Erich Raeder inspect the new warship Scharnhorst *in October 1936. The Nazis ignored Versailles Treaty limitations on shipbuilding.*

neighbours. Meanwhile Britain and Italy were suspicious of a French alliance with the Soviet Union, France was angered by an Anglo–German naval agreement, and both France and Britain condemned Italy's invasion of Abyssinia. The invasion effectively marked the end of both the Stresa Front and the League of Nations, which proved powerless to prevent Italy's aggression.

With Germany openly rearming and its opposition fractured, Hitler made his next move. To protect France and the Low Countries, the Versailles Treaty had created a demilitarized zone in the Rhineland, German territory west and east of the Rhine River. The Rhineland's status had been confirmed by the Locarno Pact of 1925, under which the Allies evacuated their troops from the area in 1930. On the morning of 7 March 1936, however, Hitler sent 22,000 troops into the Rhineland.

Hitler's move was a gamble. He had promised his generals that he would withdraw if the French opposed him. The French did nothing, however, partly because they overestimated German strength and partly because they were waiting for support from Britain. The British, however, remained suspicious of France's alliance with the Soviet Union, and also underestimated the significance of the move.

BRITAIN AND FRANCE 1937–39

A frequent question about the 1930s is why the French and British did not make a stronger stand against Hitler. Both had their own reasons for caution. France, on Germany's border, had a smaller population and economy than its neighbour, and would not be able to defeat Germany alone. The French tried to make alliances with other European states, but would still need British support to win a war against Germany. For its part, Britain faced different problems. The British Empire was increasingly difficult to defend, particularly in East Asia, where Japan was growing in strength. However, a deeper reason for French and British reluctance to confront Hitler was that both countries had been traumatized by the losses of World War I, and were desperate to avoid another European conflict.

Hitler and Mussolini

The failure of the democracies to prevent remilitarization of the Rhineland marked a great strategic victory for Hitler and for Europe's dictatorships. In July 1936, Mussolini acknowledged Hitler's claim to treat Austria as a German state. In October, Mussolini and Hitler formed the Rome–Berlin Axis, and in November, Germany and Japan signed an Anti-Comintern Pact directed against the Soviet Union.

> "The Rhineland marked a great strategic victory for Adolf Hitler"

Meanwhile, Germany and Italy both supported Francisco Franco's Nationalists in the civil war that broke out in Spain in July 1936. The right-wing Nationalists were opposed by the Republicans, government forces, workers' militias, and brigades made up of volunteers from around the world. The war lasted three years before the Nationalist victory in March 1939.

Mussolini supplied 70,000 troops, plus tanks, artillery and aircraft, to aid the Nationalists. Hitler sent fewer men but some 100 aircraft; the pilots used the conflict to perfect the techniques that would be vital in the Blitzkrieg tactics Germany employed in World War II.

The Rome–Berlin Axis opened the way for Hitler's next step after remilitarizing the Rhineland: the *Anschluss*. After the failed Nazi coup in Austria in 1934, Kurt von Schuschnigg had become chancellor with the support of Mussolini Hitler made no secret of his determination to

Austrian Nazis in the town of Graz celebrate the Anschluss *with Germany in March 1938.*

THE ANTI-COMINTERN PACT

In November 1936, Germany and Japan signed an agreement known as the Anti-Comintern Pact. It agreed that each country would help the other if either were attacked by the Soviet Union. The pact took its name from the Comintern, or Communist International. That was a Soviet committee set up in Moscow to coordinate the activities of Communist parties around the world in the attempt to create a global revolution. Italy, which had signed a treaty of friendship with Germany, joined the agreement in 1937. The effect of the pact was therefore to bring together the three chief aggressor countries that would be described as the Axis powers during World War II.

achieve the *Anschluss*, however, and the loss of Italian protection left Schuschnigg very vulnerable.

In February 1938, Hitler gave Schuschnigg an ultimatum: if he refused to include Nazis in his government, German forces would invade Austria. With no backing from the Western democracies, the Austrian initially agreed, but then announced a plebiscite to be held to re-assert Austria's independence. During the confused period that followed, Arthur Seyss-Inquart, the leader of the Austrian Nazis, forced Schuschnigg to resign. At Hitler's insistence, Seyss-Inquart became chancellor. He then invited German troops into Austria.

On 13 March 1938, Hitler declared Austria a province of the German Reich, or empire. About a month later 99.7 percent of the Austrian people voted in favour of the *Anschluss*.

Czechoslovakia

The French and British had again failed to prevent German expansion. For many Britons, especially, this policy of appeasement was a genuine attempt to resolve German grievances. They saw Hitler's aim to bring together all Germans under German government as an expression of the principle of self-determination, for example. They believed that Hitler would cease when he had achieved his aims. The French, meanwhile, were more suspicious of Hitler but were reluctant to act without British support.

The democracies' failure to resist his demands encouraged Hitler to further expansion. This time his target was the Sudetenland, a border area of Czechoslovakia that contained a large minority of Germans. Hitler used the Sudeten Germans as a pretext to claim the whole of Czechoslovakia.

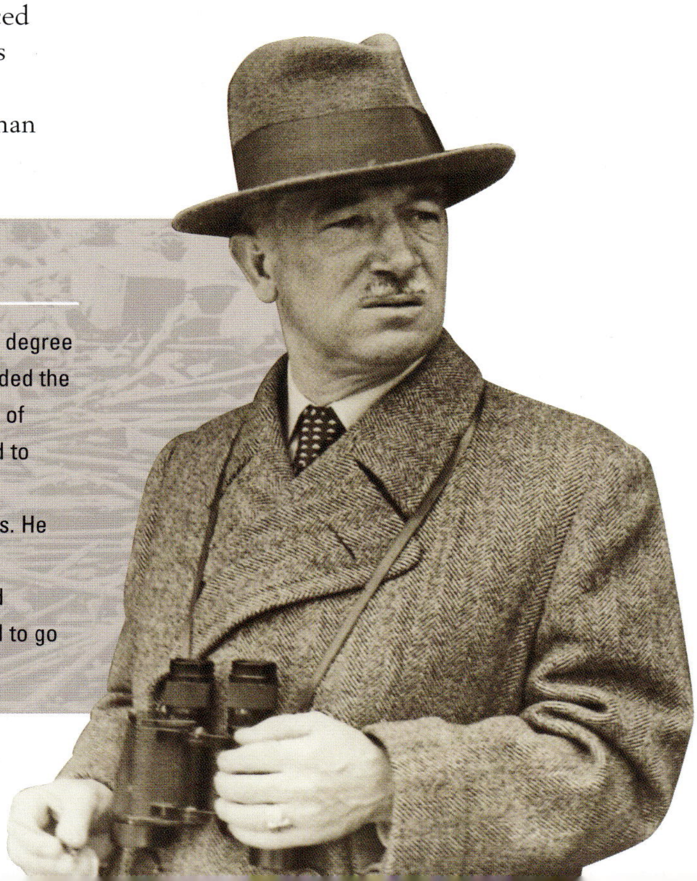

Without French and British support, Czech president Eduard Benes had little choice but to give in to Hitler's demands.

APPEASEMENT

Appeasement was the policy adopted by Britain, and to a lesser degree by France, towards Hitler's demands. Many British people regarded the Versailles Treaty as unfair towards Germany; they felt that some of Hitler's demands were just. By meeting his demands, they hoped to prevent him from making demands that risked another conflict. However, Hitler saw appeasement as weakness in his opponents. He followed each demand with another. After the occupation of Czechoslovakia, the policy lost much of its support in Britain and France. Leading politicians realized that they had to be prepared to go to war to stop Hitler.

In April 1938, under orders from Hitler, the leader of the Nazis in the Sudetenland, Konrad Henlein, began to demand self government for the Sudeten Germans. The Czech Government of Eduard Benes reacted with alarm; it called up its reservists and positioned troops along the German border. Hitler condemned what he called Czech provocation, and told his generals to prepare an invasion plan for October.

Again Britain and France chose not to resist Hitler's demands. British prime minister Neville Chamberlain had already told the French that he thought the Czechs should be prepared to give up territory. As the British and French convinced Benes to make concessions, however, so Hitler increased his demands. On 12 September, he

Mussolini and Hitler, at left, face Chamberlain (right, next to a translator) in Munich in September 1938. The Italians, Germans, British and French decided the fate of Czechoslovakia without inviting the Czechs to the talks.

NEVILLE CHAMBERLAIN

Neville Chamberlain, Britain's prime minister in the approach to war, began a career in local politics in 1911. He joined the Conservative Party and was elected to Parliament in 1918. Chamberlain served as minister of health and chancellor of the exchequer before he became prime minister in 1937. In foreign policy Chamberlain followed a policy of appeasement, and has been widely criticized since for underestimating Hitler's territorial ambitions. Chamberlain himself had an intense dislike of criticism, and did not welcome advisers who advocated different policies from his own. After appeasement failed he acknowledged that war was inevitable, and reluctantly took Britain into the conflict. Chamberlain died in 1940.

Sudeten Germans salute as German troops enter Friedland on 3 October 1938. Despite Czech concessions to the Sudeten Germans, Hitler pushed them to demand full self-determination.

demanded self-determination for the Sudeten Germans and massed his troops on the border.

Fearing war as imminent, Chamberlain called a conference at Munich on 30 September 1938, to discuss the crisis. The talks were attended by Britain, France, Italy and Germany. The Czechs were not invited. Hitler got his way: the Czechs were told to evacuate the Sudetenland by 10 October. If they did not, they would get no help to resist German aggression. Chamberlain claimed that the agreement promised "peace for our time". Within a year, however, Europe was at war.

The Munich agreement has become a notorious example of appeasement, a policy now widely discredited as naive and cowardly. Many historians believe that Hitler outwitted his opponents; Hitler himself came to the same conclusion. However, both Britain and France quickened their own rearmament. Hitler's assumption that they would not fight, based on what happened at Munich, would eventually lead him to overstep their patience.

After Munich

The Munich Agreement marked the beginning of the end of Czech independence. Czechoslovakia's other minorities, such as Slovakians and Ruthenians, demanded independence. With Hitler's support, Hungary seized territory in the south of the country. On 15 March 1939, Germany occupied the rest of the country. That same month Hitler forced Lithuania, on the Baltic coast, to hand the city of Memel – formerly part of the German state of Prussia – to Germany.

STALIN AND THE EUROPEAN CRISIS

Wary of German expansion, Soviet leader Joseph Stalin was ready to use force to save Czechoslovakia in 1938. He would not intervene without support from France and Britain, however, and it was not forthcoming. The Western powers treated the Soviet Union as a threat rather than an ally, preferring to send diplomats rather than senior politicians to negotiate with Stalin.

Western suspicions of the Soviet Union seemed well founded. Under Stalin, Soviet military and industrial power had grown considerably. The state had taken control of the economy, forbidding some forms of economic activity and imposing a series of Five Year Plans (the first was from 1928 to 1933) to increase industrial output. Meanwhile Stalin had consolidated his control of the state and become effectively a dictator. In the late 1930s he launched a series of purges to eliminate thousands of real and perceived opponents, including former Bolsheviks and experienced army officers. The loss of so many skilled leaders would greatly weaken the Red Army.

Italian Bersaglieri prepare to advance during the April 1939 occupation of Albania.

Hitler's renewed expansion in Czechoslovakia forced the Allies to recognize that his ambitions could not be appeased. Chamberlain warned that Britain's reluctance to fight did not mean that it would not fight. As war appeared inevitable, France and Britain made overtures to Germany and Italy, respectively, to buy time to rearm and to halt expansion, but such moves achieved little.

The question of Poland

On 7 April 1939, Mussolini launched an invasion of Albania. The Italian dictator had expansionist ambitions of his own, and had declared an Italian empire after the invasion of Ethiopia in 1935. After World War I, Italy had expanded its territories along the Adriatic, the sea that separated it from the Balkans; now the Balkan state of Albania was a logical target.

Mussolini's territorial expansion was easily achieved. The invasion force of 100,000 troops and 400 aircraft soon overcame the Albanian Army. The Albanian king, Zog, went into exile and Mussolini offered the crown to the Italian king, Victor Emmanuel III.

Hitler, meanwhile, turned to what he termed "the Polish question". Modern Poland had been created by the peace

Nazi banners decorate the main street of Danzig. Declared a Polish-administered Free City by the Versailles Treaty, Danzig was home to many Germans who embraced Hitler's promise to reclaim the city for Germany.

Eyewitness Report:

"Danzig is a German city and it wishes to return to Germany. I am not a democratic statesman; I am a realistic National Socialist. However, I held it equally necessary to point out to the government in Warsaw that, just as it desires access to the sea, Germany desires access to its province in the east. These are indeed difficult questions. Germany bears no responsibility for this. The ones to be blamed are the magicians of Versailles who either out of malice or thoughtlessness set up a hundred powder kegs."

Adolf Hitler, commenting on the Danzig situation, April 1939

treaties of 1919, and included two areas that between them were home to about a million Germans. The Baltic port of Danzig (Gdansk in Polish) was to be a Free City under League of Nations protection, while a narrow stretch of land known as the Polish Corridor linked Poland to Danzig and the sea, splitting Germany from its state of East Prussia.

When he had begun his policy of expansion, Hitler largely left Poland alone, signing a nonaggression pact with it in 1934. He reassured the Poles that he had no designs on their territory. After the events in Czechoslovakia, however, such promises did not seem worth very much. In October 1938, Hitler proposed building a German-controlled road across the Polish Corridor and passing Danzig back to Germany. He offered to guarantee Poland's borders in return. The Poles instead signed a pact with the Soviet Union, their eastern neighbour. The Poles also made warlike noises about fighting to prevent loss of territory to Germany.

Motorized German troops advance into Poland. The invasion was an early triumph for the fast-moving Blitzkrieg tactics the Germans used widely and to great effect.

Protecting Poland

Poland's determination coincided with the acceptance in the Western democracies that they had to make a stand against Nazi aggression. Britain and France offered to guarantee Polish independence. In the event of German aggression, they were committed to military action on Poland's behalf. Some historians question whether the allies were really prepared to fight in March 1939, or whether they were trying to warn Hitler off. Whatever their intentions, Hitler's chief concern lay in the east, where the Soviet Union could move troops into Poland far more easily than Britain or France.

Hitler wanted to avoid facing a possible alliance of the Soviet Union, Britain, and France. The Western democracies were equally aware of the Soviets' potential to deter German expansion, but their negotiations with Stalin failed.

At the same time, however, Hitler had set aside his ideological differences with

German troops remove a barrier at a border crossing during the invasion of Poland on 1 September 1939.

Stalin in the hopes of making an alliance. In August 1939 he offered Stalin a deal: if the Soviets allowed Germany to attack western Poland, they would have a free hand in eastern Poland, the Baltic states (Lithuania, Latvia and Estonia) and Bessarabia in Romania.

Approaches to Stalin

Munich had had an important effect on Stalin, who had been prepared to go to war to protect Czechoslovakia. The capitulation of France and Britain to Hitler's demands convinced Stalin that they would be unreliable allies. He decided that he had to cope with German expansion eastwards on his own, without their help. He was in continued negotiations with Britain and France during the summer of 1939, but the mutual suspicion between the Soviet dictator and the diplomats from the western democracies meant that there was no deal on the table that either side could accept.

In late August 1939, German foreign secretary Joachim von Ribbentrop visited Moscow to sign a German–Soviet Nonaggression Pact, which included the deal over territory. The agreement between two nations at opposite political extremes – fascism on one side, communism on the other – shocked the

From 1936 to August 1939, Hitler followed a policy of expansion that succeeded in creating a larger Germany without provoking war with Britain and France.

HOME FRONT

The Outbreak of War

At the outbreak of war in 1914, Britain had been a jingoistic nation, confident of victory in a short campaign. In 1939, things were different, and the nation realized the new conflict would be long and hard.

Most British people had been greatly relieved that war had not broken out during the Munich crisis of 1938. They had memories of the horrors of World War I, and many felt that Germany had been badly treated in the Versailles Treaty of 1919. However, Hitler's occupation of the remainder of Czechoslovakia early in 1939 made most realize that war was inevitable: that it was the only way of stopping Hitler's seemingly limitless territorial ambitions.

Far left: Enlisting in the Air Training Corps. It was clear that air power would be very important in the coming war.

Left: Hoardings placed around the statue of Eros in Piccadilly in April 1939, appealing for recruits. By this stage, the British people realised that war with Nazi Germany was probably inevitable.

Above: Soon after the outbreak of war, the programme of evacuating children from Britain's cities out into the countryside began. There was fear that cities would be destroyed by bombing.

Below: There was also fear of poison gas being dropped by aircraft. This photo was taken well before the actual outbreak of hostilities.

Below left: Troops drilling on the beaches of southern England in early 1939.

Western world. It also left Hitler with a free hand in Poland, which was now terribly vulnerable, and meant that war was inevitable.

The war begins

Hitler now needed an excuse to invade Poland before the Poles and their allies could make more defensive preparations. On 31 August, SS troops in Polish uniforms staged a mock raid on a radio station in the German border town of Gleiwitz. They left behind the bodies of 10 or so murdered concentration camp inmates in Polish uniforms.

Hitler used the apparent "Polish" raid as an excuse to invade Poland on 1

> “SS troops in Polish uniforms staged a mock raid”

September 1939. On 3 September, France and Britain declared war on Germany. World War II had begun.

The policy of appeasement that the Western democracies had undertaken from 1936 to 1938 had failed utterly. The British and French governments had completely underestimated the ambitions of Adolf Hitler, and had assumed that he would be satisfied with a rearrangement of the Versailles Treaty. They did not realize that they were effectively dealing with a madman whose aims would get bigger as he went from success to success. For much of the 1930s, they had been more fearful of international communism than of international fascism. The result was that Britain and France went to war in 1939 in an impossible attempt to defend the state of Poland, which was already doomed.

Chapter 3
Blitzkrieg in Poland

When German troops began streaming across the Polish border at 04:45 hours on the morning of 1 September 1939, they set off a chain of events that engulfed the world in a war that lasted for six years.

Previous pages: Vehicles of a German panzer division in Poland in September 1939.

Between September 1939 and June 1940, Germany launched a series of spectacular military offensives. The first attack was against Poland and was code-named Operation White. The German invasion force deployed two army groups made up of 55 divisions, each containing about 15,000 men. Army Group North invaded southwards from East Prussia and eastwards from Pomerania. The larger Army Group South attacked eastward from Silesia and Germany's ally, Slovakia. The German Air Force, or Luftwaffe, deployed over 1800 aircraft.

Polish forces

Against the German forces were 30 Polish divisions of about 12,000 troops each. Not all of them were mobilized on 1 September. Those that were mobilized were positioned along Poland's borders, rather than on natural defences such as the wide rivers within the country, in order to protect Poland's important industrial centres. The Polish forces were very exposed, as some parts of Poland were surrounded on three sides by German territory. The Polish air force had 1900 aircraft, but of these 650 were trainers and 700 were outdated. Most would be destroyed on the ground on the first day of the war.

German tanks in Poland in September 1939. The front tank is a Panzer I, while those behind are Panzer IIs.

> "The Luftwaffe took control of the skies within a few days"

On 1 September 1939, the Germans began air, land and sea attacks against Polish positions. Special forces teams were put ahead of the attack troops to sabotage telephone lines, blow up bridges and spread confusion. During the first few days of the offensive the German forces inflicted heavy casualties on Polish frontline units and disrupted enemy supply and communication networks such as roads and railways.

Germany advances

The Luftwaffe took control of the skies within a few days. German Stuka dive-bombers roamed deep behind Polish lines, machine-gunning and bombing columns of reserve troops heading for the front. German panzer divisions were sent into action against weak spots in the Polish line. Instead of fighting against the main defensive positions, they pushed behind enemy lines, aiming to capture key bridges over Poland's rivers. In the confusion, hundreds of thousands of refugees fled their homes, clogging up roads and making it difficult for the Polish to build up organized resistance.

The German and Polish infantry divisions fought dogged battles over the

LIGHTNING WAR

During World War I (1914–1918) there were long periods of stalemate (deadlock), as soldiers took cover in lines of trenches. If they tried to leave the trenches to attack the enemy, they were shot down by enemy machine guns. During the 1930s German and British officers realized that using tanks offered a more effective way of waging war. Tanks had been invented during World War I, but by the 1930s had become much faster and more reliable.

German officers, notably Heinz Guderian, believed that tanks could do more than break through a first line of defence. With their own support and supplies, tanks could penetrate deep into enemy territory, ruining enemy command and control, and ensuring final victory.

From this theory developed the idea that breaking through frontline defences and creating confusion behind the enemy lines could be achieved in other ways, not just with tanks. Airborne troops, such as a paratroopers, could be deployed.

This method of waging war by concentrating on the attack was known in German as Blitzkrieg, or "Lightning War" in English. Against the other European armies, German Blitzkrieg tactics were highly successful and allowed Hitler to dominate the continent.

Eyewitness Report:

"Very soon after that, menacing, dark bombers appeared in the blue sky over Chelm. My wife and I left the store and ran to the fields to hide. We wanted to hide in the tall wheat, but the wheat had just been harvested and we were exposed. We were terrified. German planes kept firing down at us with their machine guns, and they seemed to shriek like wild animals as they dived with their bombs and bullets. We decided to run home, and we made our way through the streets filled with panic-stricken people who were shrieking hysterically. When we arrived home, we found the old woman we had hired under the bed, holding our infant girl, Pesha, in her arms. She was so petrified that she was speechless. When the bombing ceased we went out on the street."

Kalmen Wewryk, Chelm, Poland, 1939

industrial regions of Krakow and Lodz. The lack of Polish motor transport had an impact on the campaign, as the Poles could not retreat faster than the Germans were advancing. As the panzer divisions defeated them and pushed deeper inside Polish territory, the Poles were left open to encirclement. After six days the Polish High Command ordered a withdrawal to the east but by then it was too late. The huge Polish armies from Posnan and Lodz were trapped around Kutno, to the west of Warsaw. The port of Danzig was quickly surrounded and cut off. German troops driving south from East Prussia had almost linked up with panzers moving up from the south, trapping Polish troops around Modlin as they did so. Only in the south was Polish resistance holding. A determined force was driving off German troops attempting to cut off the Poles' route to Romania. Romania was a potential ally and a possible entry point for Allied aid.

The trapped Polish troops at Kutno tried to make a dramatic breakout across the Bzura River to freedom. For two days the Polish kept attacking, only to be

A German horse-drawn supply column crosses a river during the invasion of Poland.

German troops remove a border marker on the Polish frontier in 1939, as Poland becomes part of the German Reich.

beaten back by German firepower, and by Luftwaffe attacks. The trapped troops resisted for three more weeks, when 170,000 Poles eventually emerged from the woods around Kutno to surrender.

By the second week of September, Warsaw was surrounded by German forces advancing from north, west and south. It held out for another two weeks as, day and night, German bombers pounded the city.

Beaten back by the Germans, Polish forces were now attacked from the East. On 17 September the Soviet dictator Joseph Stalin ordered his Red Army to cross into eastern Poland. He claimed that he wanted to prevent "anarchy" caused by the collapse of the Polish government. In fact, Germany and the Soviet Union had secretly agreed to divide up Poland between them in the

First Weeks of War

As war broke out, the British people had to get used to a new way of life, in which many things had changed utterly.

PAGE 1.—MEAT.

Consumer's Name (BLOCK LETTERS) HIS MAJESTY THE KING

Address (BLOCK LETTERS) BUCKINGHAM PALACE

LONDON. S.W.1 CA 570011

Date 16 January 1940

TRAVELLER R.B. 3.

War meant that the British people had to accept many intrusions on their privacy, and were unable to behave as they had done in the past. In particular, food was rationed. Everything anyone did had to be for the good of the country.

Left: The ration card of King George VI. The ruler of the country was happy to undergo many of the same restrictions as his subjects.

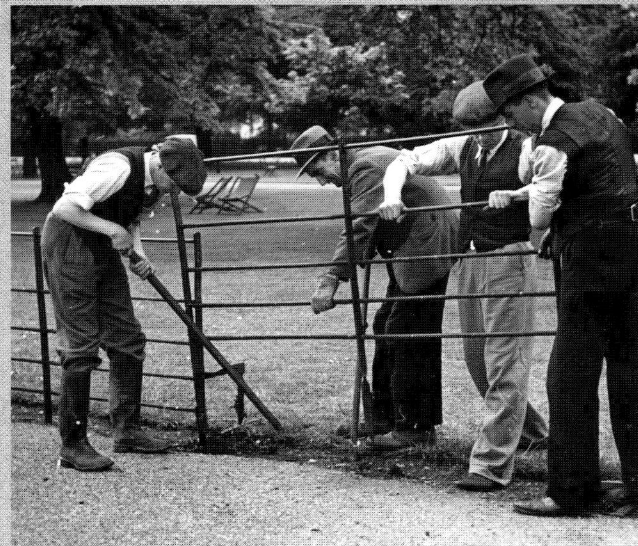

Right: Iron railings in Hyde Park, London, being torn up to be sent away to be smelted down into war material.

Right above: A ration card is checked at a grocer's store. Rationing was often irksome, and a flourishing black market in certain goods soon grew up.

Centre right: Crockery received by the Woman's Voluntary Service for use in the war effort.

Below right: Another important aspect of wartime life was the blackout, which also affected motorists.

Below: Digging for victory? Members of a family at work on their allotment.

German–Soviet Nonaggression Pact signed in the previous month. Thousands of Soviet troops poured across the border and raced west to link up with German troops advancing east.

Poland collapses

Organized Polish resistance to the invaders collapsed. In the last week of September Polish troops in Modlin and Warsaw surrendered to the Germans. A small garrison of 4500 men held out on the Hel Peninsula near Danzig until 2 October. Some 694,000 Polish troops were rounded up by the victorious Germans, and more than 217,000 Poles were seized by the Red Army. Both the Germans and Soviets treated the Poles

> “100,000 Poles managed to escape to Romania”

with great brutality. Stalin ordered most of his prisoners deported to the gulag (a system of brutal labour camps) and later had thousands of Poles executed in secret at Katyn Wood in Russia.

Some 100,000 Poles managed to escape into Romania, from where they made their way to Britain and France. A Polish government-in-exile was set up in London, and many Poles joined the British armed forces. The Germans and Soviets divided up Poland, absorbing it between their countries. A new government was set up around Warsaw and run by Nazi party chiefs. They ordered the executions of Jews, intellectuals and anyone who might rally resistance to German rule. As far as Hitler and Stalin were concerned, Poland had ceased to exist.

Chapter 4

Phoney War and Winter War

Both during and after the rapid Nazi conquest of Poland in September 1939, there was little serious fighting in Western Europe. In November 1939, however, a major war broke out in northern Europe, when the Soviet Union invaded its neighbour, Finland.

The British and French, who had declared war on Germany on 3 September 1939, had expected the Poles to hold on long enough in order for them to organize a large-scale offensive against Germany. The first Allied attack against German-held territory was the so-called Saar Offensive of 8 September. Nine French divisions made a half-hearted attack into the Saarland, an area on the French-German border between the Rhine and Moselle rivers. The operation soon halted in the face of robust German defences. The British Expeditionary Force (BEF) landed in France on 9 September in preparation for an offensive, but its armoured division was not ready for action until spring 1940.

The British and French were stunned by the speed of the German conquest of Poland. With no obvious way in which to influence the fighting in Poland, Paris and London simply ordered their armies to remain on the defensive. In fact, after the occupation of Poland there was a seven-month lull in which very little fighting took place on land. The period was nicknamed the "Phoney War", a phrase originally used by a US senator. To the Germans it was the *Sitzkrieg* (the sitting down war) and to the French the *drole de guerre* (joke of a war). British and French commanders concentrated on building up the strength of their forces, in case they were needed to come to the aid of neutral Belgium and the Netherlands, which were also under the threat of a Nazi attack. In the winter of 1939–1940 both the German and Allied sides also conducted reconnaissance flights over enemy territory. British aircraft bombed German naval bases, but were careful not to attack built-up civilian areas.

Rations and evacuees

One of the major activities of the British government as the war broke out was to evacuate children from cities to the countryside. During the 1930s, British scientists and military planners had estimated that cities would be extremely vulnerable to bombing from the air, and had planned a huge operation to move children out. There were originally plans

Previous pages: Finnish machine gunners prepare for action during the Winter War against the Soviet Union.

Soldiers of the 13th/18th Royal Hussars near Vimy in France during the Phoney War. The British Expeditionary Force was the first army to be totally motorised: all its troops could be moved by vehicles.

The British war minister, Leslie Hore-Belisha, in civilian clothes in the centre of the photo, visiting British troops in November 1939. The commander of the British Expeditionary Force, General Lord Gort, is on the right.

to move over four million children, but, in the event, one-and-a-half million young people were moved within a month of the war breaking out. Many then moved back early in 1940 as the bombing did not materialise. However, the events of late 1940, the so-called

"Gas masks were issued amid fears of terror attacks"

Blitz, showed that the estimates of bomb damage, although overstated, had not been entirely wrong. In France, too, many children were moved into the countryside, although on nothing like the scale of the British mass evacuation.

Over the winter of 1939 and into 1940, the British and French began to convert their economies to a war footing. The governments of both these countries introduced food rationing and started preparations in case of German bombing attacks on towns and cities. To protect London's population, air-raid shelters were dug in gardens and underground subway stations were prepared for use as shelters during air raids. Gas masks were issued amid fears of terror attacks with chemical weapons. For the time being, none of this occurred.

Meanwhile Adolf Hitler saw no need to place the German economy on such a war footing, since blitzkrieg was designed to bring victory in a short space of time, avoiding total war. Only 10,000 Germans had been killed in the invasion of Poland, a figure that seemed very low for such a

THE ROYAL NAVY

The Royal Navy was, in 1939, the largest naval force in the world. The massive fleet consisted of 15 battleships, seven aircraft carriers, 66 cruisers, 184 destroyers, and a huge number of support vessels. The main naval base at Scapa Flow was considered to be impregnable and dominated the passage between the North Sea and the Atlantic Ocean. Additionally there were navies controlled by British Dominions (the Royal Australian Navy, the Royal Canadian Navy and so on). However, although impressive in terms of size, the Royal Navy in 1939 had several weaknesses. Many of the battleships were old, and air power was limited to short-range aircraft. The biggest weakness, however, was strategic overstretch. The navy was required to protect British possessions world-wide, and, although in 1939 the main threat was undoubtedly from Germany, the Admiralty was acutely aware that if Japan entered the war, the British Empire in the Far East would be terribly vulnerable. This indeed proved to be the case when Japan attacked in 1941.

NO TRIUMPHALISM

The mood at the opening of World War II was very different from that at the outbreak of World War I in 1914. At the beginning of World War I Europeans had enthusiastically marched to war unaware of what was in store. The massive blood-letting of the Western Front during World War I had left deep scars on the European people. As a result, in the interwar years opposition to war, or pacifist, movements were strong. Visions of future wars with cities devastated by bombing and gas attack further fuelled unease about what a new war would herald. When Britain and France finally resolved to fight Germany after the invasion of Poland in 1939, the mood among the Allies was gloomy.

dramatic victory. Although conscription had been in force in Germany since 1935, the removal of men from the workforce into the military had so far not affected the German economy adversely.

Although there was little action on land during the Phoney War, the war was active at sea. Both Germany and Britain had a strategy that placed great emphasis on naval operations. The British plan was to blockade Germany and deprive it of essential raw materials from abroad. The German plan was to do the same against Britain. The British plan relied on the massive strength of the Royal Navy in surface vessels. The problem with this strategy was that much of Germany's raw materials actually came from within Europe. The only sea lane that would have made a significant difference was that across the Baltic and down the Norwegian coast, by which Swedish iron ore was exported to Germany. Sweden was neutral, however (as was Norway), and only in spring 1940 did the British seriously consider cutting this source of raw materials to Germany, and this was to have serious consequences.

The German strategy of attempting to cut British links with its sources of raw

November 1939: British troops take over Fort de Sainghain, on the Belgian frontier, part of the impressive French frontier defences.

materials had more substance, for Britain relied enormously on sea-borne imports from the rest of the world. The principal German hope for cutting these imports was to be via submarine warfare, using its submarine (U-boat) fleet to attack and sink merchant vessels. This had also been a prime German aim in World War I.

The problem with the German strategy was that U-boats had restricted access to the Atlantic, as they first had to cross the North Sea and English Channel, coming under threat from the Royal Navy there, especially as, at this stage, submarines could not travel far underwater.

British troops help with farm work during November 1939, when there was little or no fighting on the Western Front.

Surface raiders

However, submarines did have some successes against merchant vessels. For example, the day that Britain declared war on Germany, 3 September 1939, a U-boat sank the liner *Athenia*. U-boats also struck two spectacular blows early in the war against Royal Navy capital ships. At sea, the aircraft carrier *Courageous* was torpedoed, while, in October 1939, the German submarine *U-47* under the command of Günther Prien made a daring raid into the main anchorage of the British fleet at Scapa Flow in the Orkney Islands to the north of Scotland. It torpedoed the Royal Navy battleship, HMS *Royal Oak*, which sank with the loss of almost 800 sailors.

The German Kriegsmarine (navy) possessed just 27 ocean-going U-boats at the outbreak of the war, however, and the number of merchantmen sunk was relatively small. Far more merchant vessels were sunk by mines. Magnetic mines had been developed, which detonated when a metal-hulled ship

The Altmark*, supply ship for the* Graf Spee*, aground in neutral Norwegian waters after being attacked by the British destroyer HMS* Cossack *on 16 February 1940. As the* Altmark *was carrying captured British seamen, the Royal Navy felt justified in attacking the German vessel, even in neutral waters.*

passed over them. It took some time for the method of demagnetising (known as degaussing) hulls to become widespread enough to counter this menace. By April 1940, 128 Allied merchant ships had been sunk by mines.

Surface raiders

The British government was also very concerned about the threat to shipping posed by surface raiders. During the interwar years, Germany had developed a number of unique warships, known as "pocket battleships". They were fast and their main armament was six 11in guns. This made them a very potent threat to anything other than a battleship. Their great weakness was that, in the quest for speed, armour had been sacrificed in their construction. There were three such ships: *Admiral Graf Spee, Admiral Scheer* and *Grossdeutschland*. In September 1939, the *Admiral Graf Spee* was in the South Atlantic. In the period up to November, she sank or captured nine British vessels, before she was found by the Royal Navy and forced to fight it out at the Battle of the River Plate, an encounter that ended disastrously for the German ship.

> "She sank or captured nine British vessels"

Although there was a Phoney War in western Europe, things were very different in northeastern Europe. Here, a very real war of great savagery took place during the winter of 1939-40. Known as the "Winter War", it was fought between Soviet Russia and its smaller western neighbour, Finland.

SPOTLIGHT

The Battle of the River Plate

The Battle of the River Plate was the first major naval engagement of World War II, and showed the Royal Navy at its finest.

On 13 December 1939, three British vessels, the heavy cruiser *Exeter* and the light cruisers *Ajax* and *Achilles,* brought the German pocket battleship *Admiral Graf Spee* to battle off the coast of Uruguay, at the mouth of the River Plate. *Exeter* was put out of action, but the *Graf Spee* was damaged and withdrew into Montevideo harbour for repairs. Wrongly believing that a major British force had been assembled, the captain of the *Graf Spee* scuttled his ship rather than face another battle with the Royal Navy.

Above: The Admiral Graf Spee *at sea before the war.*

Below left: British cruisers heading towards Montevideo harbour on 17 December, expecting further combat with the German surface raider. Graf Spee *was allowed only four days for making repairs in the neutral port of Montevideo, before coming out again to face the Royal Navy. The British deceived the Germans into believing a large task force had been assembled off Montevideo.*

Left: Hearing that the Graf Spee *had been scuttled. British sailors cram the foredeck of* HMS Achilles *to witness the fate of the enemy.*

Below: The Graf Spee *burning after having been scuttled and set alight. Her captain, Hans Langsdorff, later shot himself.*

Right: The funeral of crewmen from the Graf Spee.

Finland and the USSR

Finland had been part of the Russian Empire since 1809. Although initially given considerable autonomy, attempts at Russification in the early twentieth century had caused very considerable resentment. So when the Bolshevik coup in Petrograd overthrew the Provisional Government in November 1917, the Finnish leadership saw the opportunity to gain their country's independence. Finland achieved independence, but only after a bitter civil war, in which German troops intervened. In 1932, the Finns signed a 10-year non-aggression pact with the Soviet Union, but relations with the communist regime were strained.

The Soviet concern was that in an effort to deflect Nazi aggression away from the West, the British might try to direct the Germans northeast into the Baltic region. This idea certainly worried Joseph Stalin, the Soviet dictator, who reckoned that, "[Finland] may well become the springboard for anti-Soviet moves from either of the bourgeois imperialist groupings." He believed that it was possible, "that they are plotting together for joint action against the USSR. Finland might be urged against us as a skirmish for a major war." Strangely, these views were not held by the Soviet Union alone; Sweden also began to worry that Finland might turn towards Germany for military help. Although these fears proved groundless, it shows that it was not only the USSR that was gripped by paranoia over Finland's possible pro-German orientation.

Soviet demands

In mid-April 1938, the second secretary of the Soviet embassy, Boris Yartsev, called on Finnish Foreign Minister Rudolf Holsti. Yartsev warned Holsti that Moscow was convinced of Germany's aggressive intent and that this would impinge on Finnish territory. He said that the Soviet Union

Finnish troops make use of a wood pile during an exercise. As the Soviets found to their great cost, Finland's soldiers were hardy, well-trained foes.

sought guarantees that Finland would not assist Germany in a future war against the Soviet Union, and that the Soviets would give Finland any help required

> "Finland achieved independence after a bitter civil war"

against Germany. Yartsev was rebuffed. The Soviets then tried again through more orthodox channels in April 1939, demanding the lease of certain islands in the Gulf of Finland in return for territory in eastern Karelia. The new Finnish foreign minister Eljas Erkko – Holsti had retired, due to ill health and the fact he had made some offensive remarks about Hitler at a diplomatic dinner in Geneva – again rejected the Soviet proposals. Holsti stated that the Soviet intention to offer automatic help would be "incompatible with the autonomy and sovereignty of Finland", and that Finland would regard "such a measure as aggression." These were harsh words and they added to Soviet unease, given that the independent Baltic states – Latvia, Lithuania and Estonia – were taking a similar stance. To make matters worse, General Halder, the Wehrmacht (German Armed Forces) chief of staff, was touring the region.

The Germans had, however, made an approach to Scandinavia that spring, offering Norway, Sweden and Finland non-aggression pacts. This was rejected in May, angering the Germans, but not mollifying the Soviets. Nonetheless, Hitler was little bothered by the stance of these countries on the periphery of Europe. His main concern was that he would not have to fight both the Western Allies, Britain and France, and the Soviet Union if his aggressive policy towards Poland resulted in war. The Soviets, meanwhile, were disappointed in their efforts to secure close military links with Britain and France. So Soviet Foreign Minister Maxim Litvinov was replaced by Vyacheslav Molotov, Stalin's right-hand man and importantly, given the Nazis' rabid anti-

Finnish troops on patrol during the Winter War. The Finns had excellent winter clothing to protect them from the cold.

SCANDINAVIAN NEUTRALITY

By the twentieth century Scandinavia had been relegated to the periphery of Europe politically as well as geographically. Denmark, newly independent Norway and Sweden all relied on a policy of neutrality in international affairs. This served them all well in World War I, and although not untouched by war – all three nations' merchant shipping fleets suffered heavily in the face of German unrestricted submarine warfare – the three countries emerged more or less unscathed. Finland seized the opportunity thrown up by the collapse of Tsarist Russia and the subsequent Bolshevik Revolution and declared her independence. Finland, like her Scandinavian neighbours, put her trust in the newly formed League of Nations for security in the postwar world of the 1920s and 1930s. As the League proved ineffectual in the face of Japanese, Italian and subsequently Nazi German aggression, the Nordic countries stated their strict neutrality and hoped the gathering storm would not break upon them.

Finnish soldiers examine Russian dead during the Winter War. The Red Army suffered 126,875 killed in four months of fighting in attacks against the Mannerheim Line.

Semitism, not Jewish like his predecessor. Stalin was thus sending a clear signal to the Germans that, having failed to find security in conjunction with the Western powers, he was willing to do a deal with the Nazis. Joachim von Ribbentrop, the German foreign minister, read the signs correctly and quickly informed Hitler that the Soviets seemed to be considering a military pact with the British and French. This was enough to push Hitler forward. He needed to be sure that the Soviets would not oppose his proposed invasion of Poland, and he needed an agreement soon, in order that the Polish campaign could be launched and finished before the winter rains.

Finland in danger

Hitler needed to move fast. By 23 August, von Ribbentrop and Molotov had signed a non-aggression pact. The pact contained a secret protocol dividing Europe into Soviet and German spheres of influence. The Baltic states and Finland were placed in Stalin's sphere. Poland was to be split down the middle and a whole series of economic measures were agreed. For Hitler it meant that he could deal with Poland without Soviet intervention, and, once he had finished with the Poles, he could turn westwards without concern to his eastern frontiers. For Stalin it meant that he could deal similarly with the Baltic states and Finland if he so chose. Germany's need for a free hand in Poland and the West had sealed Finland's fate.

On 17 September 1939 the Red Army occupied much of eastern Poland, and at the beginning of October the Soviets forced Estonia, Lithuania and Latvia to cede military bases on their territories to the USSR. The Finns were summoned to Moscow to discuss "concrete questions" on

JOSEPH STALIN

The dictator of the Soviet Union was not radically different from Adolf Hitler. Both men shared a dislike of liberalism and weakness, and both saw treason and incompetence everywhere. Unlike Hitler, Stalin had not seen service in Wold war I (he was found to be unfit for military service by the Russian authorities). He was happy to give a certain latitude to his generals, secure in the knowledge that his secret police maintained an iron grip over the Soviet people and that he could always have incompetent officers shot or sent to the Gulag (the system of labour camps) if they failed in their duty to Mother Russia.

Like Hitler, Stalin was utterly indifferent to human suffering, once stating: "One death is a tragedy, one million is a statistic". When his beloved wife Ekaterina died of typhus in 1908, he reportedly said, "and with her died my last warm feelings for all human beings". His brutality was legendary: in the 1930s his efforts at collectivization resulted in the deaths of up to 10 million peasants through starvation.

When Germany invaded the Soviet Union in June 1941, Stalin was initially stunned, but very quickly recovered to conduct the Russian war effort. He directed the Soviet military through the Headquarters of the Main Command (*Shtab vierhovnogo komandovani* – Stavka) as commander-in-chief, supported by army officers and commissars. Stalin rarely left the Kremlin or ventured outside the USSR.

He viewed the Western Allies with suspicion, often accusing them of postponing the second front because they wanted to see the USSR "bled white". Stalin insisted that the British and Americans adhere strictly to the repatriation terms of the Yalta Agreement, which they did, even though they knew that the policy of repatriation would mean death or imprisonment for those who were returned to the Soviet Union. Thus, between 1945 and 1947, 2,272,000 Soviet citizens were returned by the Western Allies to the USSR. One-fifth of these were either shot or given 25-year sentences in the Gulag.

5 October 1939. The Finnish negotiators headed by Juho Paasakivi were given very little leeway, and on 13 October Paasakivi was forced to reject the Soviet demand for a lease on the port of Hanko to be used as a military base, the movement of the frontier on the Karelian Isthmus westwards by some 70km (43 miles), and cession of certain islands in the Gulf of Finland in return for large areas of Eastern Karelia. A second and third round of talks achieved nothing before discussions broke down irretrievably on 13 November. It was clear Finland could expect no support from outside, while several high-ranking Germans had argued that Finland should acquiesce to the Soviet demands.

Eyewitness Report:

"I have fought on many a battlefield, but never have I seen such warriors as you. I am as proud of you as if you were my own children; I am as proud of the man from the northern fells as of the son of Ostrobothnia's plains, of the Karelian forests, the hills of Savo, the fertile fields of Häme and Satakunta, the leafy glades of Uusimaa and Varsinais-Suomi. I am equally proud of the sacrifice of the factory worker and the poor crofter as of that of the wealthy. A place of honour has also been earned by the thousands of workers who, often as volunteers and during air raids, have worked on their machines."

Marshal Mannerheim, Finnish headquarters, 14 March 1940

Finnish troops on watch during the Winter War. Thanks to expert training and good clothing, cases of frostbite were virtually unknown among Finnish soldiers.

The Winter War begins

Negotiations having failed, Stalin resolved to settle the matter by military force. It is clear that he expected the campaign to be over quickly, in much the same way that the Germans had defeated Poland. Some officers of the Red Army urged caution, but the prevailing view was that Finland would be defeated in 10 to 12 days. Given the vast disparity in forces, this was not an entirely unreasonable assumption. The Finnish Army numbered 30,000 men; it was ill-equipped with regard to modern mechanized weapons such as tanks and aircraft. The Soviet commander, General Kirill Meretskov, had 600,000 troops (the Red Army would eventually commit 1,200,000 men), supported by 1500 tanks and 3000 aircraft. However, the Finns were well led and motivated, and familiar with the terrain and conditions. The same cannot be said of the Red Army, whose officer corps had been decimated after Stalin's recent purges.

The Finns fight back

After a staged border incident, Meretskov's forces rolled over the Finnish frontier in six widely separated advances spread over a 1400km (868-mile) front. Given the inhospitable nature of most of the frontier, the Finnish commander-in-chief, Gustaf Mannerheim, was able to concentrate the bulk of his forces on the Karelian Isthmus. Here, 20,000 men dug in behind the Mannerheim Line – a series of fieldworks stretching across the isthmus – and then held off the main Soviet advance force of some 180,000 men through most of December. So solid was the resistance that Mannerheim did not have to commit his reserves. On 27 December the Soviets broke off this offensive.

However, the Soviet push north of Lake Ladoga was larger than Mannerheim had anticipated, and he was forced to draw on his reserves to stabilize that situation. In the far north, the Soviets easily captured the port of Petsamo but failed to push farther south. By late December the Finns were able to move onto the offensive: spectacular victories were secured by Colonel Talvela at Tolvajärvi on 24 December and by Colonel Siialasvuo at Suomassalmi in early January, where, with the strength of roughly a brigade, he destroyed two crack Soviet divisions. These successes convinced some in the Finnish Government that the war was winnable, although Mannerheim was always aware that the strategic situation remained grim. But these events did at least provoke a change in Soviet policy.

The Soviets abandoned their plan to put in place a puppet regime under the veteran Finnish communist Otto Kuusinen, and

Finnish ski troops such as these inflicted many casualties on the Red Army during the Winter War. Frostbite and hunger added to the Soviets' woes.

continuous contact was then established between the two governments from 29 January 1940. The Finnish bargaining position was strengthened by the interest that Britain and France were now taking in the conflict. The Western Allies had at once condemned the Soviet invasion of Finland and were much heartened by the difficulties in which the Red Army found itself. Indeed, the British also hoped that the Finnish-Soviet War, or Winter War, might also embarrass the Germans. To quote the British ambassador in Paris, Oliver Harvey, "no German except an absolute extremist can feel anything but acute discomfort at seeing the Russians attack the Finns – the Nordic race par excellence – whose independence was originally won by German aid."

SOVIET-GERMAN TRADE PACT

In February 1940 Germany and the USSR concluded a new trade pact. Under the terms of the agreement, which was to cover a period of 27 months, the Soviets promised to deliver the following goods in the first 12-month period: 1,016,000 tonnes (1,000,000 tons) of vegetables and grain for cattle; 914,000 tonnes (900,000 tons) of mineral oil; 508,000 tonnes (500,000 tons) of phosphates; 101,600 tonnes (100,000 tons) of cotton; 101,600 tonnes (100,000 tons) of chrome ore; 508,000 tonnes (500,000 tons) of iron ore; 304,800 tonnes (300,000 tons) of scrap iron and pig iron; and 2400kg (5280lb) of platinum. In return, the Germans undertook to deliver to the Soviets various industrial products, industrial processes and installations, as well as war matériel. Furthermore, the Soviet Union declared her willingness to act as a buyer of metals and raw materials in third-party countries for the German war effort. Ironically, Soviet metal ore would be used to produce many of the bombs that were used in the Battle of Britain in 1940.

The Allies look north

The British and French had expected a German offensive on the Western Front within weeks of the outbreak of war in 1939. When it failed to materialize, they found themselves looking north towards Scandinavia as a means of breaking the deadlock. Germany obtained well over half its iron ore imports from northern Sweden. There was a "growing belief in Swedish iron ore as the Achilles' heel of the German war economy." It was the unexpectedly resolute Finnish resistance to the Soviet invasion that provided the Allies with the opportunity to intervene in Scandinavia and to block Swedish iron ore supplies to Germany under the pretext of aiding the Finns. In early February 1940, the British and French governments made the decision to send an expeditionary force to Scandinavia, ostensibly to help Finland. However, this force would land at Narvik in Norway, and seize the iron ore mines in northern Sweden before providing any military support to the Finns. This plan required at the very least the acquiescence of the Norwegians and Swedes, which was extremely unlikely to be granted, given the two countries' determined neutrality, yet British preparations went ahead throughout February and early March 1940. However, activation of the plan required an appeal by Finland for help.

The Finns were desperate for military matériel, and although the free world expressed its admiration and sympathy for Finland, very little practical aid was forthcoming. Sweden, although refusing to intervene in the war, did at least sell Finland considerable quantities of arms and supplies, and allowed some 8000 men to volunteer to fight for Finland. Germany, however, remained strictly neutral. This was very much in line with Hitler's belief that Germany would not become involved in a Soviet-Finnish war. Indeed, he was somewhat scornful: "I have no great regard for countries of the North. Ever since I came to power, the papers of Sweden, Norway and Finland have vied with one another in insulting me personally ... I have truly no reason to feel any friendship towards countries whose press have treated me with such

Soviet forces in Finland dismantle anti-tank obstacles positioned along the Mannerheim Line in the Karelian Isthmus.

indignity. As for Finland, seeing that Germany in 1918, through Von der Goltz's expedition, helped Finland out of a difficult spot, I should think that we are entitled to expect greater gratitude and consideration than we have been accorded."

German hostility

By now, the Germans had even blocked the passage of Italian aid to the Finns and had refused to even honour Finnish arms orders placed before the outbreak of war. When the new Finnish foreign minister, Väino Tanner, questioned the German minister in Helsinki, Wipert von Blücher, he similarly criticized Finland for its ingratitude regarding the events of 1918 and its current "downright unfriendly" attitude towards Germany. He warned Tanner that Germany would not allow the Allies to secure bases in the north and that such a concession would be a *casus belli* for Germany. Otherwise, Germany's attitude was: "Germany has no part in the Finnish War." He certainly rejected Tanner's suggestion that Germany might approach the Soviet Union with regards to opening peace negotiations.

Meanwhile, the Soviets had also reorganized their military capabilities. Meretskov was replaced by the far more capable Semyon Timoshenko. The Red Army was reinforced, and an intensive training programme was developed using close co-operation between infantry, tanks, artillery and aircraft. During late February and early March 1940 Timoshenko was able to deliver mass tank, air and artillery attacks on the Mannerheim Line until he broke it. Once through, he made for Viipuri, which he captured on 11 March. Mannerheim, seeing the position was

Finnish ski troops were especially useful in disrupting Soviet lines of communication.

FIGHTING IN THE ARCTIC

The land and seas of the Arctic Circle are among the most inhospitable places on the planet. During World War II, they were a battlefield on a scale beyond anything that region had previously witnessed. The climate in northern Scandinavia is harsh and unforgiving, and makes the most extreme demands on military operations. For example, soldiers must contend with the dangers of the environment as well of those from enemy action. A whole host of physical problems must be overcome. In winter, some of the hazards are obvious, such as hypothermia, dehydration, snow blindness and even sunburn. There is also a very serious possibility of freezing to death in temperatures that regularly reach minus 40 degrees. The wind-chill factor increases the chance of frostbite, and heat transference may result in flesh sticking to metallic parts of weapons and vehicles. The latter require special oils, higher rates of maintenance, and there is an increased demand for fuel for both heating and transport – engines must be turned over regularly or even kept running constantly. Soldiers operating in these climates also require a higher calorific intake.

Soviet commander Marshal Semyon Timoshenko was given substantial reinforcements with which to breach the Mannerheim Line in Finland.

Finnish troops near the front during the Winter War. Note their winter uniforms.

hopeless, advised his government to make peace. The Finns debated whether to accept British and French offers of aid, but rightly considered that such help would be of extremely limited value and thus they decided to sue for peace. A delegation flew to Moscow and signed the peace treaty on 13 March 1940. Hostilities ceased the following day. The Finns were forced to cede the Karelian Isthmus, their second city of Viipuri, areas west and north of Lake Ladoga and a 30-year lease on the Hanko Peninsula to the USSR. The Winter War was over.

Facing the consequences

The implications of the Winter War were serious for Scandinavia. The Anglo-French intervention plan had shown Hitler their evident interest in the north. He therefore ordered plans for a full-scale invasion of Norway. As to the results of the war, there were two key issues.

Firstly, the Soviet Union had won a dangerous victory. Finland was deeply embittered and extremely hostile towards the USSR, and would take the first chance to have its revenge. Thus Finland would react positively when Hitler suggested a new war against the Soviets, 18 months later. Without the Winter War, Germany would have still invaded the Soviet Union in 1941, but the invasion would have been planned differently and would not have included the Finns. Secondly, the poor performance of Soviet troops gave Hitler the impression that the Red Army could easily be defeated in a war with Germany.

MARSHAL SEMYON TIMOSHENKO

In January 1940, Marshal Semyon Timoshenko (1895–1970) was given command of the Soviet armies fighting in Finland. The Soviet invasion had begun the previous November, but the advance had become bogged down by stubborn Finnish resistance along the defensive Mannerheim Line. Timoshenko demanded substantial reinforcements from Stalin and deployed them into Western Karelia, ordering an all-out assault . On 1 February 1940, blanket bombing began, and, in one day, Soviet artillery poured more than 600,000 shells onto the Mannerheim Line's positions at Summa. The decisive battle began on 6 February 1940, along a 5-mile (8km) front in Western Karelia, into which Timoshenko hurled three divisions of troops, supported by 150 tanks and 200 aircraft. By 11 February, the Soviet Red Army had succeeded in breaking through the Mannerheim Line on the Karelian Isthmus. From that point, Soviet victory became inevitable, prompting Finland to sue for peace in March. Timoshenko's reputation was greatly enhanced and he was made the People's Commissar for Defence and a Marshal of the Soviet Union in May 1940. He would go on to play an important role in World War II. He later said of his experiences in The Winter War: "The Russians have learned much in this hard war, in which the Finns fought with heroism."

Chapter 5

Invasion of Norway

The first attacks of the great German offensive into Western Europe took place against Denmark and Norway on 9 April 1940. Denmark was unable to put up any effective defence, but the German invasion of Norway involved heavy fighting. At sea and in the north around the Norwegian port of Narvik, German military forces almost faced a humiliating defeat before eventually emerging victorious.

In late 1939, Adolf Hitler ordered a study for a possible invasion of Norway. General Jodl, Chief of Operations at *Oberkommando der Wehrmacht* (OKW – Armed Forces High Command), noted that it should be carried out with the "smallest possible staff". The OKW had a first draft ready on 20 January 1940, and Hitler then ordered a *Sonderstab* (special staff) to prepare plans for the operation, to be codenamed *Weserübung* (Weser Exercise). At this stage, the plans were purely academic, yet this changed with the boarding by the Royal Navy of the German supply ship *Altmark* in Jössingfjord, Norway, on 16 February 1940, and the liberation of 303 Allied seamen being held on board.

The German plan

OKW planning gained new impetus, as Hitler was now convinced the British were about to intervene in Norway. He feared that an Allied invasion of Scandinavia would open up the Baltic Sea and Germany's undefended Baltic coast to the Royal Navy, and thus cut Germany off from its vital Swedish iron ore supplies.

OKW's plan involved occupying Denmark to provide forward air bases for the Luftwaffe. It was to be a very audacious operation. The first echelon would consist of six groups attacking the six main objectives: Group I "Narvik": 2000 men of the 3rd *Gebirgs* (Mountain) Division in 10 destroyers, escorted by battlecruisers *Scharnhorst* and *Gneisenau*; Group II "Trondheim": 1700 men in four destroyers escorted by the heavy cruiser *Admiral Hipper*; Group III "Bergen": 1300 men on two destroyers escorted by the light cruisers *Köln* and *Königsberg*; Groups IV and V "Kristiansand" and "Egersund": with the cruiser *Karlsruhe*, the depot ship *Tsing Tau*, three torpedo boats and four minesweepers; and Group VI

Previous pages: German troops in action in Norway on 24 April 1940.

With the Norwegian capital city, Oslo, now secured, the Germans could reinforce their forces in Norway. These troops have just been landed at Oslo harbour on 24 April 1940.

One of Dietl's men of the 139th Gebirgsjäger *Regiment, which fought bravely at Narvik in April and May 1940.*

"Oslo": with the spearhead of the 163rd Division, the general staff and the Gestapo, aboard cruisers *Blücher*, *Lützow* and *Emden*, escorted by three destroyers.

On 28 February Hitler approved the plan but specified that *Weserübung* must not clash with *Plan Gelb*, the offensive against Holland, Belgium and France. The commander of the Norwegian operation, General von Falkenhorst, was therefore restricted in the number of airborne troops he could deploy, while General Halder, the OKH chief of staff, who was largely unaware of the plans, only grudgingly released the mountain troops von Falkenhorst asked for. Luftwaffe commander Hermann Göring was enraged that airborne units had been put under Falkenhorst's command, but his protests to were to no avail. The navy at least was more enthusiastic.

On 3 March Hitler decided to launch *Weserübung* before *Gelb*. As the British and French frantically tried to persuade Finland to accept aid in the days before the Finns signed the ceasefire with the Soviets, Hitler considered launching the operation early to forestall the Allies. The Peace of Moscow concluded between the Finns and Soviets, however, allowed for preparations to proceed at a calmer pace, and on 7 March, Hitler formally authorized the use of land forces in the operation.

Early on 7 April Admiral Lütjens, the naval commander of *Weserübung*, ordered his flagship, Gneisenau, to leave the port of Wilhelmshaven with the rest of Group I for Narvik, while Group II headed for Trondheim. Lütjens' force was spotted by

THE SEA WAR OFF NORWAY

Apart from airborne units, the German troops that landed in Norway all had to be transported by sea. The Norwegian campaign involved heavy fighting for the German Navy. An attempted landing near Oslo on 9 April, for example, was opposed by Norwegian shore batteries and the cruiser *Blücher* was sunk. On 10 April the German cruiser *Karlsruhe* was successfully attacked by British Skua dive-bombers. Separately, the British battleship HMS *Rodney* damaged the battle cruiser *Gneisenau*.

Further north, during the fighting for the port of Narvik, there were two separate battles involving German and British destroyers on 10 and 13 April. In the first engagement each side lost two destroyers, but many German supply vessels were also sunk. In the second battle of Narvik, the battleship HMS *Warspite* with a destroyer escort sank eight German destroyers. During the evacuation of Allied forces, the German navy could take comfort from sinking the aircraft carrier HMS *Glorious* and its destroyer escorts

However, the Royal Navy could easily absorb its losses; the German Kriegsmarine, however, never fully recovered from its losses in surface vessels during the Norwegian campaign.

French Alpine troops make a dramatic landing in Norway from a ship. However, their performance in battle in Norway was less spectacular.

The German invasion of Norway in 1940. German forces landed at several ports simultaneously, largely taking the Norwegians by surprise.

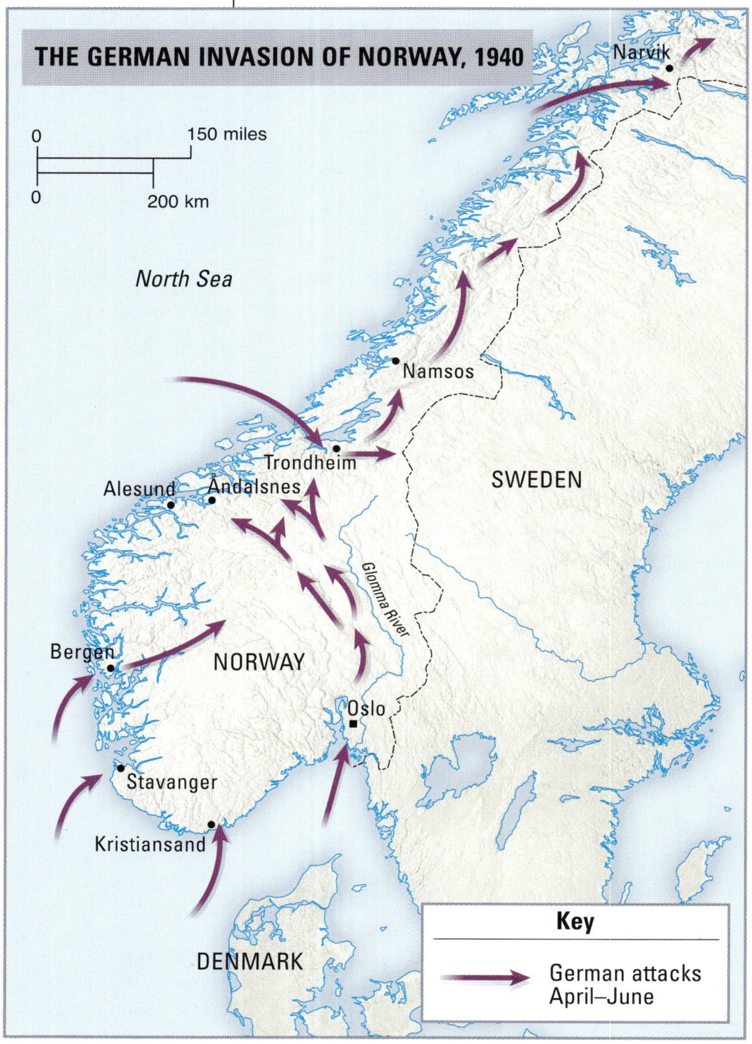

Royal Air Force (RAF) Coastal Command aircraft, but the British Admiralty did not believe the German ships were heading for Norway. Rather, it was felt they were planning to break out into the Atlantic and attack merchant shipping. To counter this, the British Home Fleet sailed from Scapa Flow, heading northeast in an effort to block the presumed German move towards the Atlantic Ocean.

The Germans land in Norway

On 9 April German troops of General Eduard Dietl's mountain division were relieved to enter the inshore waters of Oforfjord, leading to Narvik's port. Dietl reported to von Falkenhorst by 08:10 hours that Narvik was in German hands.

At Trondheim the forts guarding the approach were taken by surprise and fired hopelessly at the passing German ships. Admiral Schumdt's Group III narrowly missed the British Home Fleet off Stavanger, and was outside Korsfjord which leads to Bergen on schedule by 02:00 hours. The Norwegian troops in Bergen quickly withdrew in good order, allowing the *Köln* to land her troops, who soon secured the city.

Group IV, however, had problems in entering Kristiansand harbour, but Captain Rieve of the *Karlsruhe* resorted to subterfuge, and at 11:00 hours the Norwegian fortress received a message in Norwegian code: "British and French destroyers coming to your help. Do not fire." It worked, and German troops managed to land and take the town.

At Oslo, the 324th Infantry Regiment, plus a full military band, had been landed by aircraft outside the city. The soldiers then made their way into Oslo, where the band held an impromptu concert in an effort to persuade the Norwegian people that the Germans were in control. Effectively they were.

It had been a successful day for the Germans. In addition to the seizure of all objectives, Denmark had fallen with barely a shot being fired. Yet not all was to go Germany's way. The British and French had just pledged Norway their support, and, even now, the British were preparing an expeditionary force. On 14 April the first British troops were landed in Norway. The day before, German troops began to push out from Oslo on three axes: east, north and west. The Germans, with powerful air support, swept aside improvised road blocks, scoring some quick successes. Between 13 and 14 April, a Norwegian regiment surrendered near Tønsberg, southwest of Oslo, and 3000 Norwegians at Kongsvinger withdrew into Sweden to avoid encirclement.

Eyewitness Report:

"Suddenly, there was a massive explosion and we could see clouds of smoke coming from the *Blücher*. Suddenly the *Blücher* listed slightly to the left, soldiers and also nurses who could be seen on board slid down into the Oslo Fjord. I stared in horror at the drama unfolding in front of me. And it didn't take long before we saw the stern of the *Blücher* rise up in the air and the bow was pressed downwards, and at that moment, a large number of fishing boats appeared from the Norwegian and Swedish shores and tried to save the men swimming around in the freezing water. The rocks sticking out of the fjord offered them some hope, but they were so slippery that the soldiers who tried to hold onto the rocks slid down and drowned unless they could be saved by the Norwegian and the Swedes. It wasn't long before we saw the *Blücher* sinking at the front and gradually take everything down into the icy depths."

Reinhold Runde, German infantryman, on the sinking of the German cruiser *Blücher* in Drøbak Sound, Norway, on 9 April 1940.

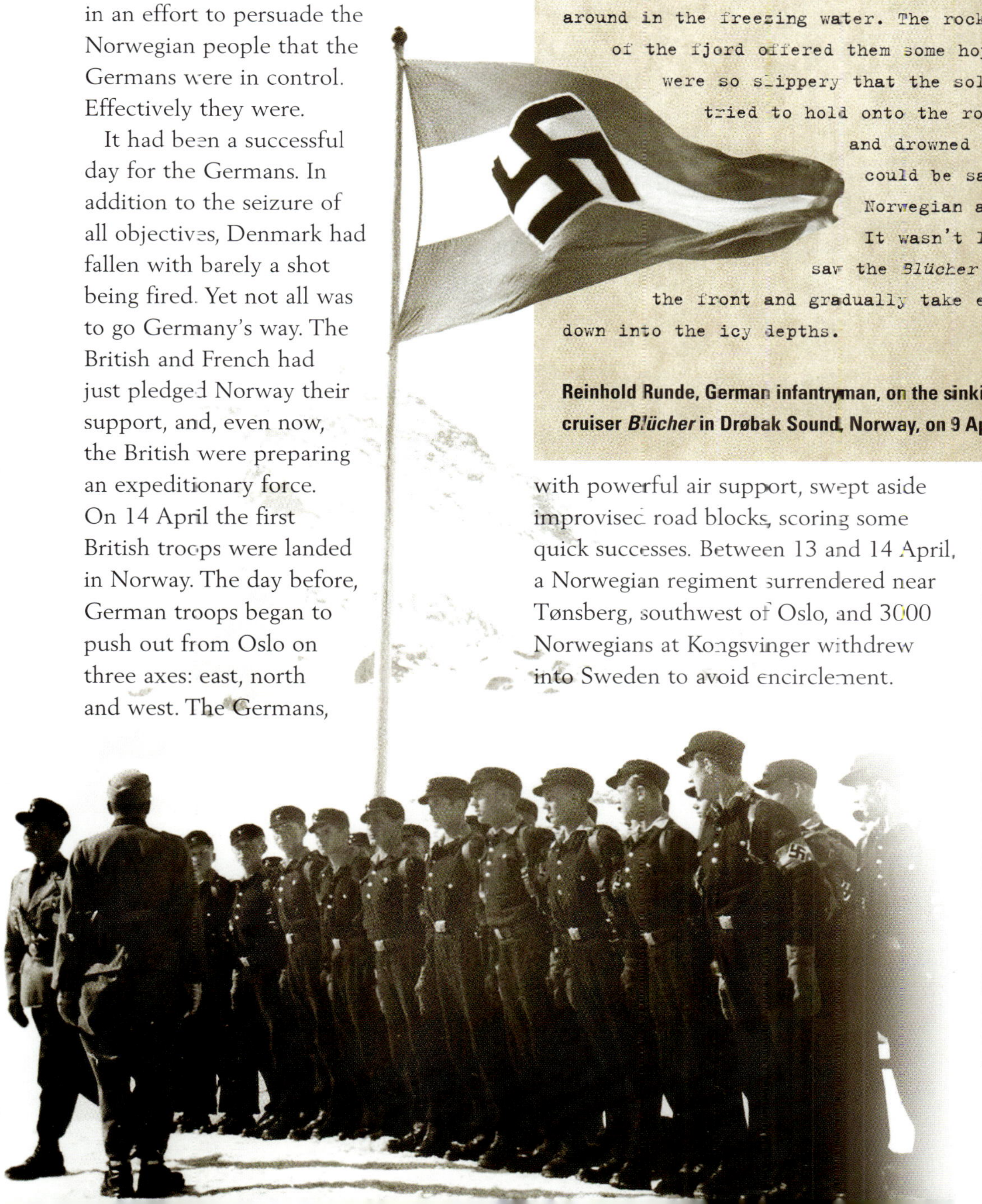

German Gebirgsjäger *(mountain troops) on parade. The 3rd* Gebirgs *Division spearheaded the German attack on Norway in 1940.*

German victory in the south

British troops landed in Norway between Andalsnes and Namsos from 14 to 19 April. On 21 April, two British battalions were mauled by three German battalions supported by aircraft, artillery and tanks. There was a brief respite for the Allies, though, as French reinforcements began to arrive, and French and Norwegian commanders even drew up a plan to attack Steinkjer. However, by 26 April, the British and French had decided to evacuate central Norway. The British evacuation was completed on 1–2 May. Remaining Norwegian forces in southern and central regions surrendered on 3 May.

In the north, British, French and Polish troops were put ashore near the German-occupied port of Narvik on 14–15 April. Thus, the situation for Dietl and his 4000 men was grim. On 9 May, two parachute companies of the 2nd Division landed near Narvik after minimal training and Dietl formed a loose defensive perimeter around the town. Hitler, in a panic, had suggested that Dietl's men be airlifted out or withdrawn south, but Jodl said such a course was impossible.

In early May, the Allies received their first tanks and landing craft. The dilatory General Mackesy finally agreed to attack German positions around Bjerkvik. On 12 May, supported by naval gunfire, French Foreign Legion troops landed on the seafront, coming under heavy fire from the German troops. However, as Allied forces attacked the Germans' rear, the French took the town, pushing on to

German troops watch the Luftwaffe reduce a British position during the fighting in Norway.

the military camp at Elvegårdsmoen, which was captured after hand-to-hand fighting. The French force then made for the Øyord Peninsula, which would provide a springboard for the assault on Narvik. The German position was grim.

British and French troops in northern Norway in April 1940. In general, Allied aid to the Norwegians was haphazard and inadequate.

Decision in France

On 10 May, the Germans put Plan *Gelb* into action and invaded France, Belgium and the Netherlands. Early German success forced the British and French to reassess their commitment to Norway. On 23 May, the British War Cabinet discussed a chiefs of staff report that recommended a total evacuation of Norway. New British prime minister, Winston Churchill, agreed, and so Auchinleck was instructed to evacuate northern Norway as quickly as possible on 25 May. However, he was also told to attack Narvik to cover the withdrawal of Allied forces and to deny future exports of iron ore to Germany by damaging Narvik's port. Covered by Royal Navy gunfire, British, French and Polish troops captured the town after bitter fighting. Despite desperate counterattacks, the Germans were being pushed back. Major Haussels had to order the evacuation of the town, and the French Foreign Legion began to push Dietl's men back towards the Swedish border. Hitler gave Dietl permission to retreat into Sweden and be interned if necessary. However, this did not prove necessary, as the British and French withdrew 11 days later on 8 June. King Haakon and his government left Norway on 7 June 1940. General Ruge, who preferred to stay with his men,

VIDKUN QUISLING

Vidkun Quisling was a Norwegian politician who rose to power during the German military conquest of Norway.

Before the invasion, Quisling, who was leader of the tiny Norwegian fascist party, made secret plans to "invite" the Nazis to occupy Norway in order to prevent British intervention. However, Adolf Hitler did not trust Quisling and ordered German troops to launch a surprise attack instead. Quisling then declared himself prime minister anyway, but his government soon collapsed. At first, the Germans did not give Quisling any power, but in 1942 they allowed his party to become Norway's only legal political organization. Quisling then imposed strict measures to crush resistance to Nazi rule in Norway. Hated by fellow Norwegians, Quisling's collaboration with the Nazis meant his name came to mean "traitor". He was executed by the Norwegians in October 1945.

SPOTLIGHT

Churchill comes to power

A major result of the campaign in Norway was the resignation of British Prime Minister Neville Chamberlain and his replacement by Winston Churchill.

During the 1930s, Winston Churchill had felt himself to be a lone voice in the wilderness, opposing the prevailing policy of appeasement towards Nazi Germany with just a small band of like-minded politicians. Many members of the Conservative Party saw him as a dangerous warmonger. When war broke out in 1939, however, Churchill was brought into the cabinet as First Lord of the Admiralty. Early in May 1940, the failure of the Allied operations in Norway led to support for Chamberlain ebbing away.

Above: Churchill during the "wilderness years" of the 1930s, when his calls for armed resistance to Hitler fell on deaf ears.

Top right and main photograph: Familiar images of Churchill during the struggle to defend Britain from invasion in the dark days of 1940, after the fall of France.

Above: Winston Churchill in 1915 in French uniform while serving as a major in the British Army on the Western Front during World War I.

Right: The young Winston Churchill. He enjoyed a successful career as a journalist before 1900.

Below: Lord Halifax, one of the politicians most closely associated with appeasement, was Churchill's main rival for the position of Prime Minister in May 1940. Already Foreign Secretary, Halifax was the preferred candidate of many Conservative MPs. He later became Britain's ambassador to the USA.

Above: One of Churchill's closest associates in his determined fight against the policy of appeasement was Anthony Eden (on left), here shown with the French finance minister in 1939.

surrendered to Dietl the following day. The campaign for Norway was over.

The British lost 4500 men, 1500 of whom were aboard the aircraft carrier HMS *Glorious* and her two destroyer escorts, which were all sunk by the *Scharnhorst* and *Gneisenau* during the evacuation. The French and Poles lost 500 men and the Norwegians about 1800. German losses were 5000. They also lost 242 aircraft, in comparison to 112 from the RAF. However, it was in terms of warships that the cost of the German victory became significant.

The Kriegsmarine lost 3 cruisers, 10 destroyers and 4 U-boats, while the *Scharnhorst* and *Gneisenau* sustained heavy damage. By the campaign's end, only one heavy and two light cruisers and four destroyers were fit for action. British losses were similar in scale, but could be easily absorbed. For the German Navy, Norway was a campaign from which its surface fleet never fully recovered.

The spoils of war

In return for these sacrifices, Germany secured the Scandinavian minerals and iron ore route. Raeder gained the bases that he wanted so much, thus loosening British control of the Atlantic approaches and making a British naval blockade of Germany more difficult. Once the Arctic convoys to the USSR began, these bases proved particularly useful. However, Norway had to be garrisoned and this proved to be a serious drain on German resources. Even the strategic importance of Norway as a naval base was lessened after the fall of France, as ports on the French west coast provided German U-boats direct access to the Atlantic.

The Norway campaign had shown the German ability to undertake combined services operations in which the Germans had proved to be far more capable than the British, although admittedly most of the British troops had been territorials.

Chapter 6
Preparing for Blitzkrieg

The Blitzkrieg stunned the world in 1939. The speed and shock of German mechanized units, supported by air power, shattered the Allied armies. But what exactly was Blitzkrieg warfare?

Blitzkrieg was a form of highly mobile warfare that depended on powerful armoured thrusts, backed by massive air support. It is the form of warfare that is still dominant today, as the invasion of Iraq in 2003 demonstrated.

Blitzkrieg warfare had its roots in World War I. The trench deadlock of that bloody conflict had been a nightmare scenario for the German Army. The problem was how to achieve a swift and decisive victory, against strong defences and massed machine guns. During World War I, the German General Staff, first under General Erich von Falkenhayn, and then under Paul von Hindenburg and Erich von Ludendorff, sought an answer by re-organizing their infantrymen. New drills were developed around small, more mobile battle groups within each infantry company. These units would use surprise in the attack: secret troop concentrations (made at night and at the last moment), and short, intense, and accurate artillery bombardments would precede the attack. The tactical unit was the squad of between 14 and 18 men, and each squad would have its own fire base – a light machine gun and mortar. Specially trained assault infantry – known as storm troops – would advance and probe the enemy for weak spots. Strongpoints would be bypassed at all costs; the overriding principle was to maintain the momentum of the attack.

Previous pages: The steel spearhead of the Blitzkrieg – German tanks and armoured personnel carriers.

New tactics

In September 1917, the German Eighth Army, commanded by General Oskar von Hutier, was outside the Russian-held

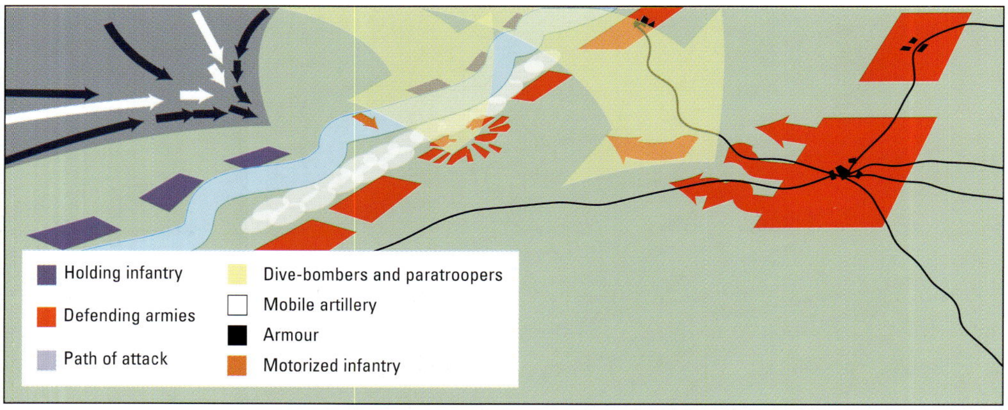

The Blitzkrieg Phase One: holding infantry engage defenders' attention along the front. As dive-bombers attack reserves and frontline artillery, German armoured spearheads, with sappers, cross the river.

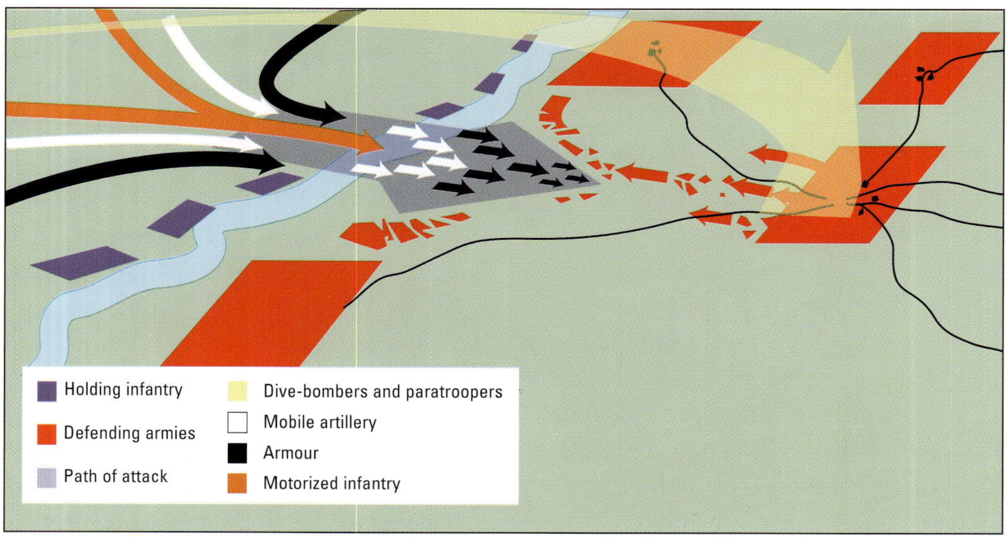

Phase Two: assault troops and demolition squads knock out enemy strongpoints and widen the bridgehead. Armour passes through them and advances into the enemy rear, followed by motorized infantry and artillery. Dive-bombers clear a path ahead.

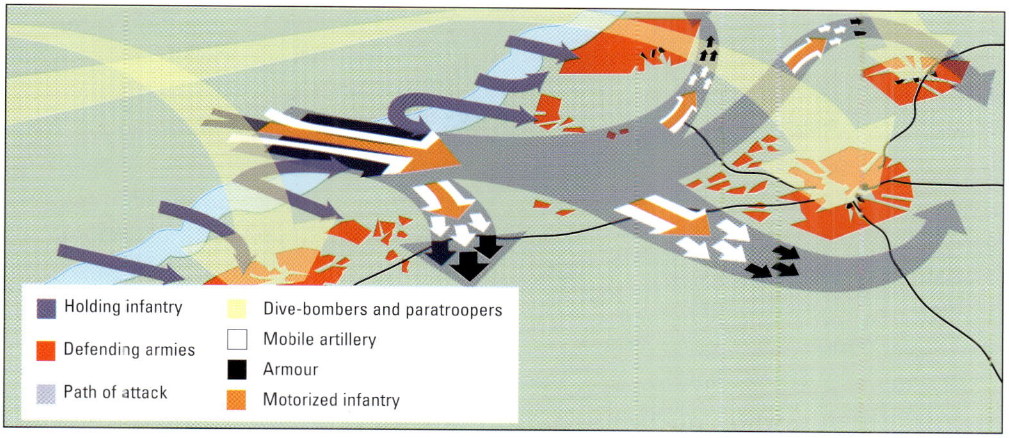

Phase Three: armoured spearheads fan out and bypass enemy strongpoints. Panzers sweep around key road and rail junctions, paralyzing enemy supply, reserve and command elements.

Phase Four: German spearheads drive deep into enemy territory as marching infantry moves up to surround and then reduce pockets.

town of Riga, which had been under siege for a considerable amount of time and had resisted all attempts to take it. Using the new tactics, Hutier attacked the town on 1 September. Following a short but intense bombardment, his infiltration units went forward. Riga fell two days later.

The new tactics were tried on a larger scale in Flanders in 1918, when Ludendorff launched Operation Michael. Beginning on 21 March, his storm troops went forward and began to achieve spectacular results. Bypassing strongpoints, they smashed through weak resistance. However, the Germans soon discovered that tactical success could not be turned into strategic victory. The army was unable to keep the advancing troops reinforced and the frontline storm troops ran out of momentum. The Allies then launched their own counteroffensive on 8 August 1918 and Germany was defeated.

In defeat, the much-reduced army of the German Weimar Republic continued to analyze what had happened. Under commander-in-chief General Hans von Seeckt, no fewer than 57 committees were established to examine the lessons of World War I. The results laid the foundations for later success.

The key way ahead lay in the exploitation of a new weapon that the British had introduced onto the World War I battlefields: the tank. The armour plate of the tank could shrug off machine-gun bullets; its caterpillar tracks enabled it to roll over enemy trenches and barbed wire; its own armament of machine guns and an artillery piece could defend it from enemy infantry and artillery; and, finally, it was very mobile, able to continue to press into the enemy rear areas faster than infantrymen could march.The tank combined the strengths of infantry, cavalry and artillery.

Theorists all over Europe began to realize the potential of tank warfare during the 1920s. In Germany, there was Ernst Volckheim, who wrote *German Tanks in the World War* in 1923 and *Tanks in Modern Warfare* a year later.

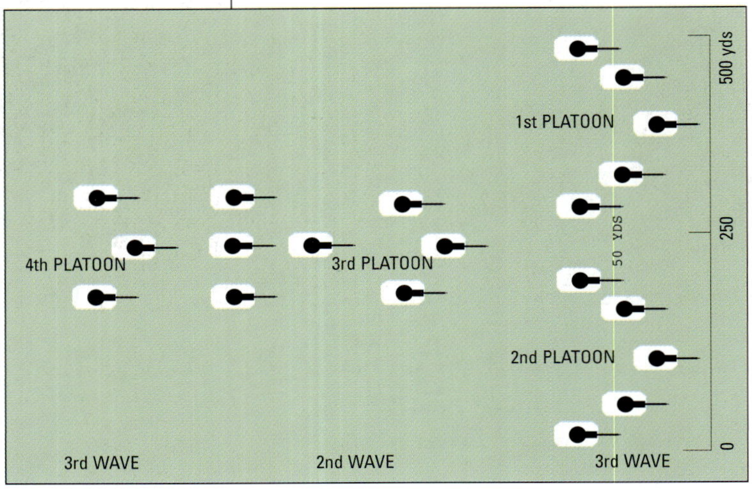

Diagrammatic representation of a panzer company in a "blunt wedge" formation. The primary mission of the panzers was to break through and attack the enemy's artillery and anti-tank guns, as opposed to his tanks.

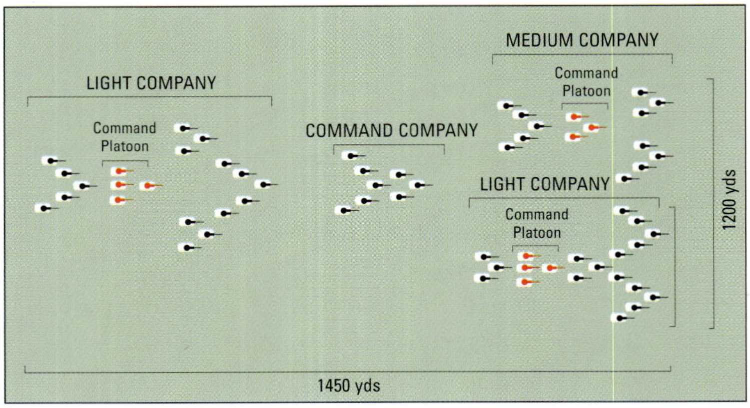

Diagrammatic representation of a panzer battalion in attack formation. The panzers aided each other by fire and movement: medium or heavy tanks (Panzer IIIs and IVs) would take up hull-down firing positions (behind obstacles or rises in the ground) to give covering fire, while the faster tanks (Panzer Is and IIs) advanced to the next commanding feature. Then the latter would give covering fire to the former moving forward to their next position.

In Britain too there was also great interest in armoured warfare, where Basil Liddell-Hart and John Fuller published work on the subject. Fuller had particular expertise, having organized the British Experimental Mechanized Force in the 1920s to test theories of mechanized warfare.

The panzer divisions

The most important aspect of the approach taken in Germany was that tank formations were to be deployed only in conjunction with motorized infantry, anti-tank guns and artillery. The focus was on concentration of armour, the use of armour in mass and the importance of surprise. To this end, a series of exercises involving dummy tank battalions took place at the Jüterbog and Grafenwöhr training grounds in 1931 and 1932.

In June 1934, a new Motorized Troops Command was created under General Oswald Lutz. Its chief of staff was General Heinz Guderian, (later known as "the father of the panzer divisions"). Guderian developed many aspects of Blitzkrieg warfare, having enthusiastically studied the writings of other armour enthusiasts. He corresponded in particular with Liddell-Hart.

Germany's first three panzer (tank) divisions were created on 15 October 1935, and Guderian was given the command of one of these divisions. There was disquiet among many more senior officers, however, about the resources Hitler was prepared to put into armoured formations. General Ludwig Beck, head of the Army General Staff, tried to have all tanks used as infantry support weapons. Guderian pressed his theories publicly with the publication of his book *Achtung! Panzer!* in 1937. He continued to grow in importance, and in 1938 was promoted to be Chief of Mobile Troops. He worked out in great

detail how panzer divisions should operate. In particular, the divisions were given extremely strong engineering units

The focus was on concentration of armour and surprise

and he made sure that their radio communications were very effective.

The crucial final piece that gave Blitzkrieg its great effectiveness began to fall into place late in the 1930s, when air power came into its own. During the Spanish Civil War, Luftwaffe pilots had had invaluable combat experience, and realized how they could work in conjunction with ground forces. The ability of the Luftwaffe to provide close air support literally added another dimension to land warfare. In particular, Ju 87 Stuka dive-bomber squadrons proved invaluable flying artillery support. The Germans also realized the importance of strong anti-aircraft units for the panzer divisions.

Air power also gave the Germans a joker in the pack in 1940: airborne troops, delivered by parachute, glider or simply flown onto enemy airfields. During the attack on Norway, such troops had enabled the Germans to take over Oslo even though sea-borne forces had struggled to reach the Norwegian capital. During the attacks on Holland and Belgium in May 1940, important strongpoints were taken by such troops.

German enthusiasm for the new opportunities offered by technology was not matched by the Western Allies. In France, for example, there had been

Motorized units on the advance in Belgium in May 1940. Halftracks were used to tow artillery, anti-tank and flak guns, which could be quickly deployed to erect a flak screen against enemy aircraft or a "Pak front" against counterattacking enemy armour. In this way, the combined-arms panzer division was a potent military formation that could react to rapidly changing tactical conditions.

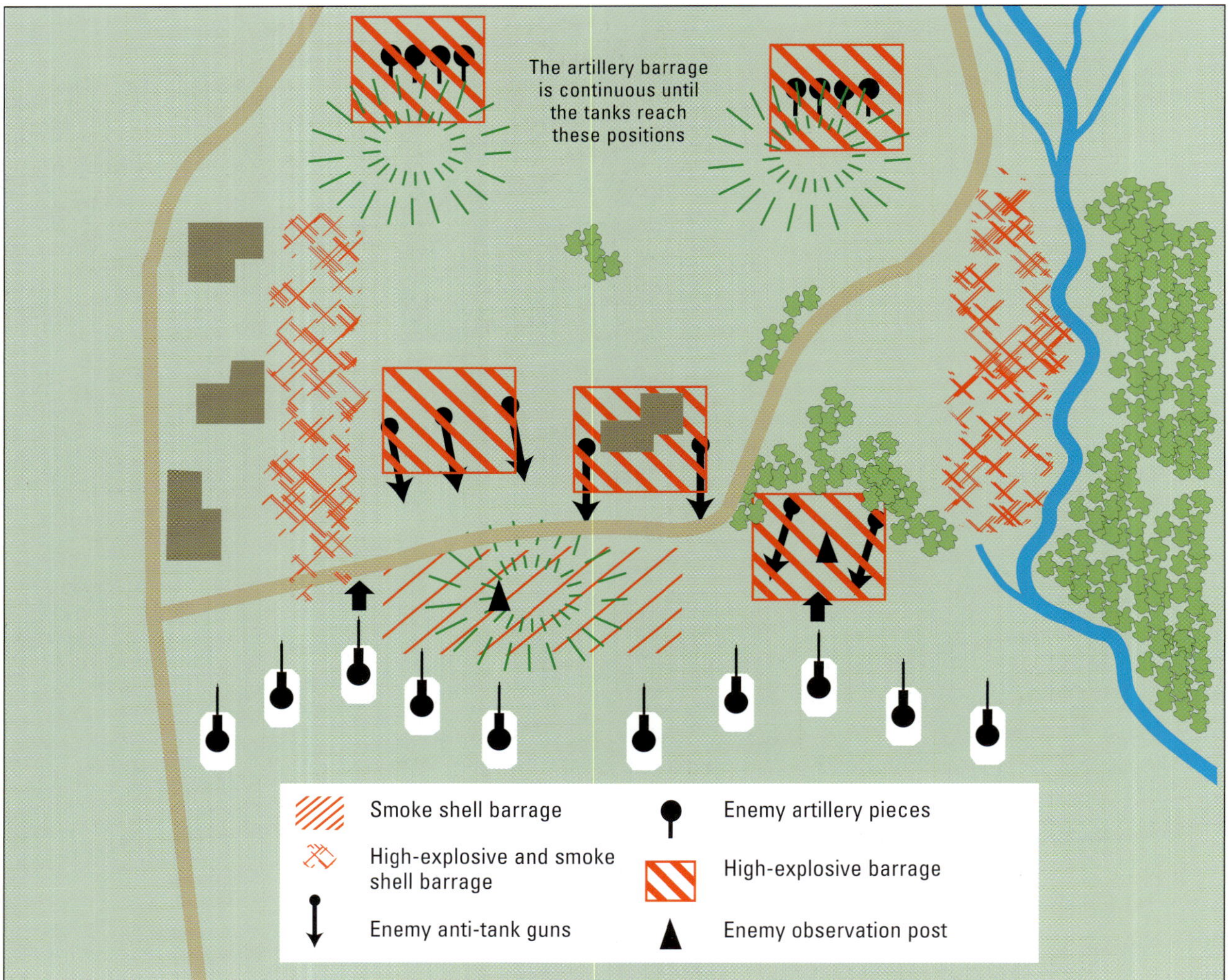

Diagrammatic representation of a panzer attack against enemy artillery and anti-tank guns. Artillery support was of decisive importance to a successful tank attack. During an assault, the missions of the artillery were: counterbattery fire, blinding enemy observation posts, engaging anti-tank defences, screening the flanks with smoke, and delaying the movement and deployment of enemy reserves, especially tanks.

many proponents of a strong tank arm from the early 1920s onwards. Lieutenant Colonel Charles de Gaulle wrote an influential book in the 1930s entitled *The Army of the Future*. He found supporters in political circles, but the industrial production of French tanks was slow during the 1930s. Most French senior officers believed (with the German General Beck) that tanks were best used as infantry support.

The difference in approach between the Western Allies and Hitler's Germany was evident during the early months of 1940. The German army planners originally came up with a scheme similar to German strategy at the start of World War I in 1914: they would attack west from Germany into neutral Belgium, then swing south into northern France to take Paris. They extended the plan to include an invasion of neutral Holland, north of Belgium, but otherwise it was predictable. The Germans did not want to attack directly across the border with France itself because the French had built massive fortifications, the Maginot Line, along the border.

Manstein's master plan

The Germans knew the Allies would be prepared for an attack through Belgium, but believed that by also invading Holland they would make an advance to the Channel coast easier and that Blitzkrieg tactics would ensure victory for the Wehrmacht. In February 1940, however, Hitler learned of a plan devised by Major-General Erich von Manstein. Manstein knew the attack into Holland and Belgium would lure the French and British armies north. So he suggested another attack with large armoured formations through the wooded hills of the Ardennes region, near Luxembourg. If these panzer divisions could cross the Meuse River near the town of Sedan, they could sweep behind the Allied forces advancing into Belgium, and destroy the Allied position.

A German anti-tank gun in France in 1940. During the Blitzkrieg, it was the anti-tank units that dealt with enemy tanks, not the panzers.

Seizing the opportunity

Some senior German officers were worried by Manstein's plan. If the panzer divisions did not cross the Meuse River very soon after the offensive began, then they would become vulnerable to air attack in the narrow valleys of the Ardennes. Hitler liked the idea, however, and planning for the operation began late in February. The plan also suited the temperament of many senior German officers, especially those who commanded the panzer divisions, and Manstein's proposal was enthusiastically supported by them.

The Allied commanders, meanwhile, were locked into their predictable move into neutral Belgium should the Germans attack. Senior British officers realized how risky this could be. British Corps commander Sir Alan Brooke noted in his diary his worries about "the danger of leaving our present prepared position for one totally unprepared and the exposure of our flank..." In spring 1940 the German High Command saw a great opportunity ahead of it, while the Allies saw only problems.

HEINZ GUDERIAN

A cavalry leader turned staff officer in World War I, Heinz Guderian was an ardent anti-communist who in 1919 served with the *Freikorps* in defence of his native East Prussia against the Bolsheviks. In 1935 Guderian took command of the 2nd Panzer Division, and then in 1937 he published his major work on armoured warfare, *Achtung! Panzer!*

After war broke out in September 1939, Guderian daringly led XIX Motorized Corps in the deepest penetration the German Army achieved in Poland. Subsequently, during May 1940, he commanded his XIX Corps in its audacious penetration of the Ardennes and its subsequent breakthrough to the coast that isolated the BEF at Dunkirk and forced its evacuation. Between June and December 1941, Guderian led the Second Panzer Group in Operation Barbarossa as it rampaged through the Soviet Union right up to the gates of Moscow. His inability to halt the enemy during the Soviet winter counterattack, however, led Hitler to dismiss him in late December 1941. Hitler recalled him during the spring of 1943. The Führer gave him unprecedented authority to reorganize and revamp the panzer arm that had been savaged during the bitter Eastern Front battles. Guderian both rationalized and dramatically expanded German armoured production to restore some of the panzer arm's lost combat power. In the spring of 1945, having quarrelled once again with his Führer, Hitler sent Guderian on extended "medical leave", bringing his wartime military career to an inglorious end. He died in 1953.

Chapter 7

The Fall of France and Dunkirk

In six weeks in 1940, the German Army defeated the combined might of the British, French, Dutch and Belgian armies in a Blitzkrieg campaign that shook the world. But the British Army was saved from destruction by the miracle of Dunkirk.

By May 1940, 2.9 million German troops and 3000 tanks had been massed along the border from the North Sea to Switzerland. They faced British and French forces totalling more than three million men with 3600 tanks; there were also about 100,000 Belgian and Dutch troops. Many Allied vehicles were better armoured and gunned than those of the Germans, but they were split up into small groups. In the air the Germans had a decisive advantage, with 3200 aircraft against 1200 French and 500 British military aircraft.

Despite Germany's success in Poland, the Allies underestimated the enemy's leadership, morale and battlefield skill. They also believed that the Maginot Line and defensive lines in Belgium would stall a German attack while an Allied counteroffensive could be launched.

Eyewitness Report:

“Manoeuvres had not prepared us for the refugees and empty houses. We did not go through big cities with our horses and artillery, but stayed in the countryside. The farms had been abandoned, and we often encountered the refugees from them. They had left their homes because they heard the sounds of battle coming towards them. Because they did not know what else to do, they had panicked and run away. It was sad to see them: women, children and old men with bicycles and horse-drawn carts loaded with whatever they could carry, going they knew not where.”

Siegfried Knappe, German soldier in France during May 1940

Opening moves

Hitler's western offensive began at dawn on 10 May 1940. The Luftwaffe attacked Belgian and Dutch airfields, and paratroopers seized key bridges and airfields. The three army groups struck at different targets. Panzer and infantry divisions from Army Group B raced into the Netherlands and Belgium while

Army Group A, led by three panzer corps, advanced to the Ardennes. Further to the south, Army Group C advanced to the Maginot Line, hoping to confuse the French as to the real aim of the German offensive.

For the Allies, and certainly for the Belgians, the most shocking aspects of this opening offensive lay in the use of paratroops and soldiers in gliders. In a dramatic assault, airborne troops in gliders landed on top of the Belgian fortress of Eben Emael and forced its surrender. Eben Emael had been a key part of the Belgian defences, with enormously thick reinforced concrete intended to withstand the heaviest artillery barrage. Yet it had no defence against a handful of infantry that audaciously landed on top of its concrete mound. The loss of the fort forced the Belgian Army to fall back to the Dyle River, to be reinforced by the British Expeditionary Force (BEF) and the French First Army. In a matter of hours, German troops were heading deep into Belgium itself, ahead of any schedule that the Allies had imagined possible.

Farther north, paratroopers landed in the Netherlands to seize a string of canal bridges in order to breach Dutch defence lines. Dutch troops pinned the attackers into small pockets, and fighting raged as

Watched by their commander Erwin Rommel (on bank in peaked cap), troops practise river crossing ahead of their invasion of France in 1940.

Previous pages: A German 88mm gun in France.

French refugees flee the Germans in June 1940. The huge number of refugees on the roads of France severely hampered troop movements.

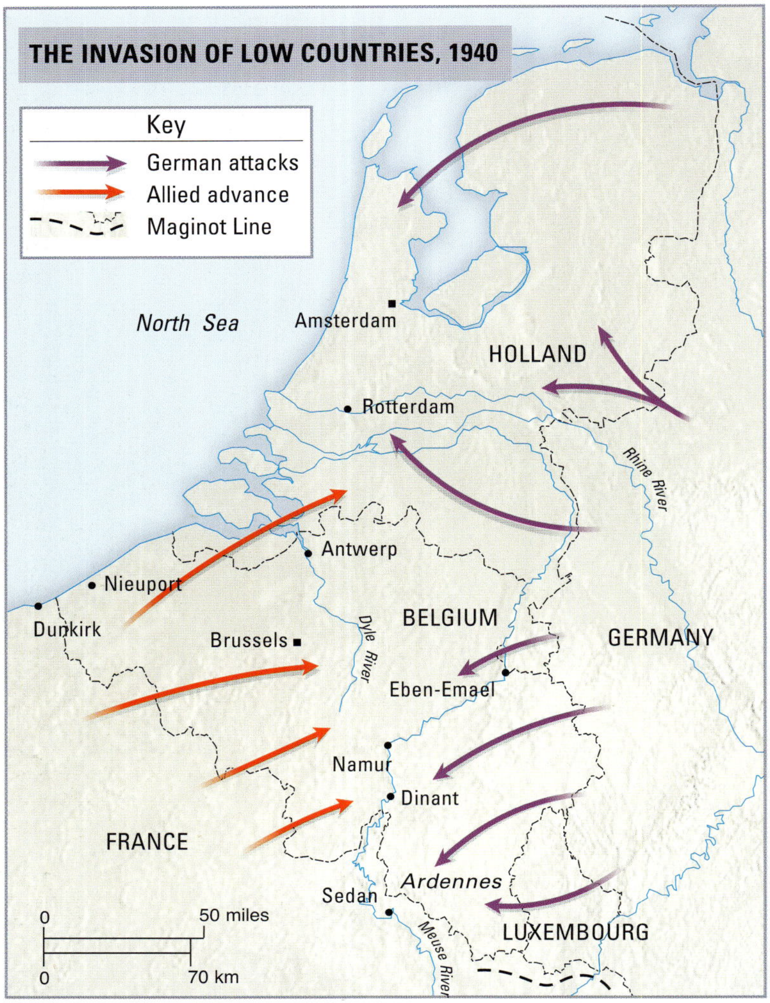

The German invasion of Holland and Belgium was made easier because of the flat terrain of the Low Countries.

The British king, Edward VI, inspects French troops during a visit to France before the German offensive.

the Germans tried to relieve the trapped men. The Dutch had some success, but the continued German advance meant that the French Seventh Army struggled to get close enough to help. With Stuka attacks making movement difficult, the French finding it hard to get into position and the Belgians unable to hold onto a fixed line of defence, by 13 May the Dutch forces were reeling. The following day, the Germans launched a huge bombing raid on Rotterdam to try to force the Dutch to surrender. Bombs flattened much of the city, making 77,000 people homeless. On 14 May, the Dutch Army surrendered. The Dutch government and navy fled to safety in England.

By 15 May, the Belgian, British and French forces, totalling some 35 divisions, had halted the German drive along the Dyle River. However, the Germans continued to fight to cross the river, and German forces were also advancing from the Netherlands.

> “The Allied command had fallen for Hitler's deception”

The fighting on the Dyle was, however, not the sector where the campaign was to be decided. The Allied command had effectively fallen for Hitler's deception; the German advance had drawn the BEF and the French First Army into Belgium. The Germans were springing their trap by pushing through the Belgian and French troops in the Ardennes. The French divisions holding the sector were reserve formations, and in fact just seven French divisions were spread out over a front of 136km (85 miles). The Allies had assumed that tanks would be useless in the heavily forested region and so these divisions were woefully badly equipped. Two divisions had only one fifth of their official allotment of anti-tank guns,

German armoured vehicles stream through the countryside during the drive towards Sedan in May 1940. The town was a key objective in the invasion of France.

while the lack of proper anti-aircraft defences meant that German Stukas were barely troubled in their attacks.

On 10 May, three German panzer corps advanced into the Ardennes, racing to reach the Meuse River on the border before the French could react. In the south was Guderian's XIX Corps with three divisions, aiming directly for Sedan; in the centre was Reinhardt's XLI Panzer Corps with two divisions; in the north was Hoth's XV Corps, aiming to cross the Meuse between Houx and Dinant, and including Erwin Rommel's 7th Panzer Divisions, which was to play a key role in the campaign.

By 12 May, General Heinz Guderian's three panzer divisions had reached Sedan

Although vulnerable to attack by enemy fighter aircraft, Stukas were a much-feared part of the German Blitzkrieg.

THE STUKA DIVE-BOMBER

With its screeching siren, the German Junkers Ju 87 dive-bomber, known as the Stuka, a short version of its full name, spread terror across Europe during the Blitzkrieg years. Stuka pilots dove down to only 915m (3000ft) to deliver their bombs accurately.

On the battlefield the Stukas closely supported panzer divisions by attacking enemy forces blocking any advance. The Stukas were known as the "flying artillery of the panzers".

German forces such as these SS troops relied on motorcycles and other forms of motorized transport to advance rapidly through France.

German paras drop on Holland in 1940. They could operate behind enemy lines for days. The Luftwaffe set up an airborne force in the 1930s. The paratroopers were trained to go straight into action on landing.

on the Meuse. The next day Guderian unleashed his artillery and tank fire on enemy defences. On 13 May, the infantry began to cross the river, supported by aircraft, artillery and tank fire.

Further north, Erwin Rommel, in command of 7th Panzer Division, urged his men on in the face of heavy fire to cross the river near Dinant. Small German engineer units crossed by boat as air attacks confused the French defenders. Gradually over the next 24 hours the German commanders got infantry and tanks across, often under heavy fire, and the French front broke. By 15 May, six panzer divisions were across the Meuse and advancing westwards into the French interior.

Race to the Channel

With the Luftwaffe in command of the air, the German tanks began to move west at maximum speed. Although the tanks quickly outran their supply lines, they were ordered to refuel from French petrol stations to keep moving.

The Allies had realized on 11 May, when their forward units in the Ardennes were forced back, that a major thrust was developing in the area, but were shocked by the speed of the German advance.

The British Royal Air Force (RAF) and French aircraft attacked the Germans in the Ardennes, but suffered heavy losses because of the excellent anti-aircraft units that were part of Germany's panzer divisions. In a four-day advance, the Germans destroyed eight Allied divisions, and had opened up a breach 128km (80 miles) wide in the Allied front.

The Allies were thrown into confusion. There was some optimism still in the Allied high command, however. Many generals could remember the German offensives of 1914 and 1918, which had ground to a halt. Winston Churchill recalled how French Premier Paul

German troops pass through the ruins of Nieuport, Belgium, in May 1940.

Tired, hungry and demoralized French prisoners are escorted to the rear by a German sentry in May 1940.

Reynaud told him by telephone on 15 May: "We have been defeated... the front is broken near Sedan; they are pouring through in great numbers with tanks and armoured cars." Churchill replied encouragingly, "I remember 21 March 1918. After five or six days they have to halt for supplies and the opportunity for counterattack is presented."

This optimism was sadly misplaced, however. The difference now was that tanks were not slow-moving infantry, nor vulnerable horsed cavalry. Provided they could find enough petrol, the tanks could carry on at a devastating rate. There was another difference, too. Whereas in World War I the defending force had been able to rush reinforcements by rail to cover a breach in its defences, in 1940 the picture was very different. The French defenders found their movements hampered by the throngs of refugees that crammed the roads, and found their road and rail columns attacked from the air. German aircraft roamed over northern France, attacking civilian as well as military targets, and making organized manoeuvres very difficult for the French.

A contemporary wrote how: "The most harrowing sight was the children... It was frightful to hear their terrified young voices screaming 'the planes, mummy, the planes!' and to know that they must already have seen death falling from the skies..."

The Allies hastily pulled forces back from Belgium and 20 Allied divisions were ordered to counterattack against the German breakthrough. To redeploy on the scale required meant that 500 trains and 30,000 vehicles had to be used

Eyewitness Report:

"There was no sound of enemy fire. We had just reached the southwest corner of the wood and were about to cross a low plantation, from which we could see the five tanks escorting the infantry below us to our left front, when suddenly we came under heavy artillery and anti-tank gunfire from the west. Shells landed all round us and my tank received two hits one after the other, the first on the upper edge of the turret and the second in the periscope."

Erwin Rommel, commander of the 7th Panzer Division, May 1940.

Troops and vehicles of a German panzer division in France in May 1940.

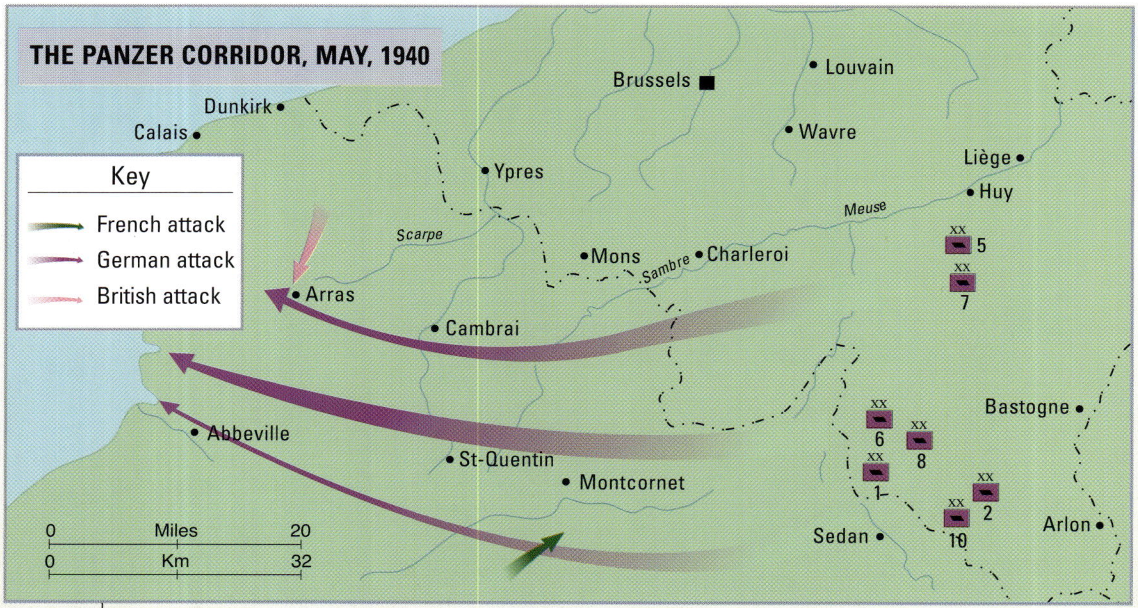

The "panzer corridor", 13–20 May. By the late afternoon of 12 May, all three German motorized corps had begun to exit the hilly Ardennes terrain and move onto the approaches to the River Meuse. This geographical feature represented the last substantial obstacle between the German armour and the open plains of central France beyond. Early on 15 May, Reinhardt's 6th and 8th Panzer Divisions successfully burst out of their bridgehead across the Meuse. By evening the corps had advanced rapidly west an incredible 50km (31 miles) to Montcornet against disintegrating French resistance. In the process, Reinhardt's armour extended north the critical hole that Guderian's armour had ripped through the French centre. These advances caused disagreements among senior German commanders (Hitler himself had grave misgivings about the speedy panzer advance). In mid-May, for example, Guderian received orders from Kleist that he exercise greater caution by slowing his advance and protecting his vulnerable flanks. Then Kleist ordered Guderian to halt, prompting the latter to tender his resignation.

and, as we have seen, the Luftwaffe attacks and the crowds of refugees made smooth transport impossible.

The main drag on the German advance was, in fact, Hitler himself, who was now nervous about a counterattack from the south. He ordered the tanks to slow down to await reinforcements, provoking rage from Guderian. His superiors managed to persuade Hitler to allow the advance to continue.

The Allies did manage some attacks on the flanks of the advancing German tanks. On 17 and 19 May, Colonel Charles de Gaulle led the French 4th Armoured Division against Guderian's forces, and succeeded in penetrating to within a mile of the German headquarters. On 21 May, British tanks struck south towards Arras, while the French launched a supporting operation. The British ground to a halt when they ran into a concentration of German tanks and anti-tank guns led by General

> "Hitler was now nervous about a counterattack"

THE LITTLE SHIPS OF DUNKIRK

As the British Expeditionary Force retreated towards Dunkirk, the Royal Navy began an operation to bring the army home. Destroyers and merchant ships began to shuttle across the Channel, but soon the docks at Dunkirk could not take all of the Allied troops crammed into the shrinking bridgehead. Navy commanders turned to a fleet of so-called "little ships", such as pleasure craft and fishing boats, to lift men off the beaches and carry them to larger ships offshore.

It had been intended to crew the little ships with Royal Navy sailors but in answer to appeals in Britain their owners volunteered to sail across the Channel. By 26 May, some 30,000 men were being lifted off the beaches each day. German aircraft machine-gunned and bombed the evacuation day and night, sinking more than 200 ships. But the operation was a success. The bravery of the volunteer crews of the little ships entered British folklore as the miracle of Dunkirk.

Allied sailors and troops take to a lifeboat after their ship was bombed and sunk off the beaches of Dunkirk.

Abandoned vehicles are strung across the beach at Dunkirk after the retreat of British troops.

SPOTLIGHT

Dunkirk

The rescue of the beleaugured BEF from the beaches of Dunkirk in 1940 seemed a miracle at the time. It kept the British Army in being.

The evacuation of Allied troops began on 27 May, and was completed by 3 June. About 300,000 soldiers were taken off the beaches, often under heavy fire, and a further 200,000 were evacuated from other ports. Although the event was token of a complete military defeat, the heroism shown during these days was a great boost to British morale. The army had been saved to fight another day.

Left: Men of the Ulster Rifles wait for evacuation on an improvised pier at Bray Dunes, near Dunkirk.

Below: Wounded troops aboard a train after landing in southern England.

Below left: An RAF Lockheed Hudson makes a reconnaissance flight over Dunkirk, as the oil tanks in the town throw up thick smoke.

Erwin Rommel. The attack shocked the already worried Hitler, however, who ordered the panzers not to press on to the lowlands near the English Channel. Hitler's "stop order" kept the panzers halted for two days, until 26 May.

The German High Command now ordered the army to focus on the Allied troops trapped in northern France. They were retreating west to the coast in the hopes of setting up a strong defensive line. In Paris politicians and military commanders sent every available man, tank, gun and plane into action to try to stop the German advance. But by now, the morale of the French Army and people was on the verge of collapse.

The British Government was equally confused, but the new prime minister, Winston Churchill, ordered the BEF to fall back to Dunkirk on the coast, where it was to be evacuated by the Royal Navy. He ordered the RAF to cut back its air support in France in order to preserve its precious fighters to defend Britain. Meanwhile, with his country all but overrun, the Belgian king surrendered on 28 May 1940.

Main photograph: Lines of hopeful troops on the beach at Dunkirk, waiting to be picked up.

Above: Some of the lucky ones, on the quayside at Dover after being carried across the English Channel.

Below: Some of the unlucky ones. British and French troops being led into captivity. In all, over one million Allied troops were taken prisoner during the battle for France. Dunkirk was a small mercy after such an enormous defeat, but mercy it was.

Retreat to Dunkirk

The withdrawal to Dunkirk was a traumatic experience for the Allied troops. By the end of May they were penned into a small bridgehead and were being shelled and bombed around the clock. However, Hitler's order to halt his panzers outside Dunkirk gave most of the trapped Allied troops a chance to escape. A fleet of civilian ships helped the Royal Navy rescue more than 220,000 British and 113,000 French troops. The Germans rounded up some 1.2 million Allied prisoners in northern France and the Low Countries, however, along with 1200 field guns, 11,000 machine guns and 75,000 military vehicles. Despite Dunkirk, the Allies had suffered a major defeat.

The Road to Dunkirk – Critical Dates

1932, July – In the national election, Hitler's NSDAP emerges as the largest party.

1933, January – Hitler becomes chancellor of Germany; he bans the Communist Party and passes legislation to give himself dictatorial powers.

1934, 30 June – "The Night of the Long Knives" sees more than 70 members of the Nazi Party murdered by order of Hitler, who believes they are a threat to his absolute authority.

1934, December – Clashes between Italian and Ethiopian forces in Italian Somaliland.

1934, December – Japan gives notice that it will no longer abide by the Washington Treaty, because it wants parity with British and US fleets.

1936, June – Civil War breaks out in Spain between Nationalists and Republican government forces. Fighting continues until 27 February, 1939, when Britain and France recognize General Franco's Nationalist regime.

1938, September – The Munich agreement, between Britain, France, Italy and Germany, promised "peace for our time".

1938, 9–10 November – *Kristallnacht* (Crystal Night) marks an intensification of anti-Semitism in Germany, as Hitler's supporters launch attacks on the Jewish community. Since 1933, half Germany's Jewish population have fled the country.

1939, March – Hitler extends his occupation of Czechoslovakia; in April, Mussolini moves into Albania.

1939, 1 September – Hitler invades Poland.

1939, 3 September – Britain and France declare war on Germany; the following day, Bomber Command launches its first attacks against Nazi warships.

1939, 7 September – France begins minor skirmishes across the border with Germany.

1939, 27 September – Polish army is unable to hold its defence of Warsaw; by the end of the month, a total of 50,000 Poles have been killed and 750,000 captured. Germany has lost 10,572 troops.

1939, November – The Winter War begins, as Stalin assembles his forces to crush the Finns.

1939, December – British cruisers engage the German battleship *Graf Spee* at the mouth of the River Plate, off Uruguay. *Graf Spee* withdraws and is eventually scuttled by her own crew.

1940, February – Finland is forced to retreat in the face of the Soviet onslaught.

1940, February – A British destroyer violates Norway's neutrality to rescue 299 British merchant seamen held on a German transport ship.

1940, 9 April – Germany begins its invasion of Norway and Denmark.

1940, May – Germany launches its invasion along the Western front into Belgium, Holland and Luxembourg, aiming to reach France. British and French forces are surprised by an Ardennes attack, which drives between Allied fighting forces.

1940, 15 May – The Dutch army capitulates after the bombing of Rotterdam. Nothing seems to be able to halt the German advance into France. The Belgians surrender on 28 May.

1940, 18 May – German forces reach the French coast south of Calais, cutting off Allied forces.

1940, 26 May – The British Expeditionary force has been driven back to Dunkirk. In Operation Dynamo, a flotilla of vessels sails across the channel to the rescue. Over 300,000 troops are brought back to England.